CAESURA ‖ LETTERS

COMPOSED BY JAMES SHELLEY

VOLUME V

WAYS OF SEEING

CAESURALETTERS.COM

CAESURA LETTERS
Volume V: Ways of Seeing

by James Shelley

Associate Editor: Cal Chayce
Idea Collaborator: Matt Ross

Front cover image: Plato's Allegory of the Cave by Jan Saenredam (1604 engraving). Colouring by Lucia Roman (2013).

International Standard Book Numbers (ISBN) associated with this title:
978-0-9732364-3-9 (Electronic book text)
978-0-9732364-2-2 (Paperback)

Caesura Letters
London, Ontario
Canada

CAESURA ‖ LETTERS

Compelling and provocative ideas.

TABLE OF CONTENTS

CAESURA ‖ LETTERS

Compelling and provocative ideas.

...a periodical for the mindfully adventurous.
...a creative resource for the life-long learner.
...a search to encounter new ways of thinking.

Join an expedition through the archives of the human imagination, from the hallowed chronicles of ancient history to the laboratories of contemporary science. Explore the origin of our ideas, trace the lineage of our inherited assumptions, and revisit the genesis of our beliefs. Journey through cultures, traditions, and disciplines of the past and present, in search of the world's most compelling and provocative ideas.

Caesura Letters subscriptions are available in multiple formats:

- Weekly letters delivered to your postal mailbox.

- Email, online, or RSS.

- Quarterly ebook.

- Quarterly paperback.

To subscribe or sign up for a free preview,
please visit **caesuraletters.com**

The Cave

Plato's Cave is perhaps the most famous and iconic analogy in the history of Western philosophy. It is presented as the third of three allegories in which Plato describes his theory of knowledge (which is closely tied to his theory of education).

He begins by using the sun as a metaphor for the illuminating power of knowledge. Just as our eyes are useless without the light of the sun, "whose light makes our vision see best and visible things to be seen," (Republic, 6.508a) so too the "domain where truth and reality shine resplendent" (508b) is "the cause of knowledge, and of truth in so far as is known." (508e)

Levels of knowledge, Plato continues, can be thought of as a continuum, as four quadrants marked along on a straight line. The first two quadrants represent our knowledge of the visible world: images in the imagination (for instance, what you visualize in your mind when you think about a house) and images of physical sight (what you see when you actually look at a house). Here, says Plato, our knowledge is simply made up of our opinions and beliefs about the world that we uncritically take for granted.

The next two quadrants represent intelligible knowledge: abstract maths (say, the theoretical architecture of house construction) and the invisible forms of ideas (what is the ideal 'concept' of a house, anyway?). This is the domain of hypothesis and dialectic. Here we seek "to get sight of those realities which can be seen only by the mind." (510e-511a) And this, says Plato, is the highest form of knowledge. Just as imaging something in your mind is different than seeing it with your eyes, so too, 'understanding' something is different than a true 'knowledge' of it.

To draw the examples of the sun and the divided line together, Plato then recounts the famous cave allegory:

> Next…compare our nature in respect of education and its lack to such an experience as this. Picture men dwelling in a sort of subterranean cavern with a long

entrance open to the light on its entire width. Conceive them as having their legs and necks fettered from childhood, so that they remain in the same spot. (7.514a)

Behind the prisoners, at the mouth of the cave, there is a fire. Between the fire and the prisoners there are puppeteers, and the light from the fire casts shadows of the puppets on the cave wall, directly in front of the bound men. Since these captives have been here since birth, the only world they have ever known is this show of shadows on the cave wall. This is Plato's lowest level of knowledge: the perception of images, for "such prisoners would deem reality to be nothing else than the shadows of the artificial objects." (7.515c)

One day, a prisoner manages to break free of his chains. The man stands up and, turning around for the first time in his life, is now able to "discern the objects whose shadows he formerly saw." Looking past the puppets, the man is "compelled to look at the light" of the fire itself. He now sees how the light was the source for creating the shadows. Finally, someone drags him out of the cave into the sunlight, where he encounters the greatest source of light, the sun, in all its radiant glory.

Thus, Plato's cave analogy represents his four levels of knowledge: First, we are held prisoners, assuming that the shadows in our mind are real (imagination). Second, our escape begins when we can see the objects/puppets as they really are (visual perception). Third, a true understanding comes only through perceiving the origin of light (the source of illumination). And, lastly, full knowledge is only achieved by discovering the sun (the highest ideal of light itself).

Plato imagined what might happen to the man if he were to return to his cave. What would his fellow detainees have to say about his account? "Would he not provoke laughter, and would it not be said of him that he had returned from his journey aloft with his eyes ruined and that it was not worth while even to attempt the ascent?" (7.517a) The escapee is ruined for cave life. His former friends are incapable of understanding him and he, having glimpsed reality, cannot rejoin their game of bestowing "prizes for the man who is quickest to make out the shadows as they pass and best able to remember their customary precedences." (7.516c)

So it is, says Plato, that once your soul ascends "to the intelligible region" and you enter the "contemplation of things above" you, too, will be ruined for a life of watching puppet shadows dance across the wall. Once you discover the light, no longer can you bear to be entertained by shadows. Once you discover knowledge, you can no longer bear to be lulled and comforted by superstitions, puppeteers, and the fables of your fellow captives.

Navigating Assumptions

Prediction

Why do we love music? Whether at a concert or sitting in our homes, music has the capacity to make us feel and experience life differently. But how does this happen? Nothing actually touches us when we listen to music, save for some invisible wavelengths impinging on our eardrums -- but yet our brains respond with all kinds of feedback and response. Musical notes, strung together in a pattern and sequence -- literally, just changing frequency patterns -- can give us feelings of great pleasure and joy. Why does this happen?

In 2011, Canadian neuroscientists Valorie Salimpoor and Robert Zatorre commenced a study to better understand how the brain reacts to music. Using brain scans (while simultaneously measuring physiological factors like heart rate, respiration, and body temperature) they demonstrated that the intense pleasure of music is correlated with heightened dopamine activity in the mesolimbic reward pathway. (Salimpoor, et al. 2011) In other words, the same mental circuitry that handles your sense of expectation, prediction, and anticipation of, say, food and drink, also seems to be aroused by sequences of musical notes floating through the air.

The researchers suggest that the reason we engage with music is because we subconsciously interact with it by predicting its movement. Music is fundamentally a pattern: it invites us in to its rhythm, syncopation, harmony, tempo, crescendo, and melodic directions. Once we are in, we engage by anticipating its next move. Music, then, excites our desire to sense what is coming. We can anticipate a song's future, feel it approach, and revel in its arrival. The researchers suggest that this explains why music is a central and cherished trait of every culture on the planet.

Consider our species' past: our ability to anticipate upcoming, hypothetical situations, strategically adapt to them, and then respond to them accordingly, is a cornerstone of what we are. We are an incredibly forward-looking, future-sensing creature. It is unsurprising, then, that we are hardwired to respond to patterns that we can predict. So much of our existence is consumed with formulating our response for what might be coming next.

For instance, just ask yourself this: How much of my efforts today are ultimately driven by the goal of making tomorrow more predictable?

BENIGN VIOLATIONS

What makes something funny? During the last couple of thousand years, numerous theories of humour have been suggested. Do we laugh because we feel superior to a situation? Or is humour simply a tension-release mechanism? Aristotle wrote,

> Comedy, as we have said, is a representation of inferior people, not indeed in the full sense of the word bad, but the laughable is a species of the base or ugly. It consists in some blunder or ugliness that does not cause pain or disaster, an obvious example being the comic mask which is ugly and distorted but not painful. (Aristotle, Poetics, 1449a)

Many theorists have suggested that humour is evoked by harmless breaches of norms and rules of behaviour. For instance, why is tickling or play fighting funny even while assault and aggression themselves are immoral? Or, why would a person who generally strives for the alleviation of human suffering find themselves laughing uproariously at the harm done to another person in a slapstick comedy sketch? Indeed, we do have a tendency to laugh in the face of danger -- or at least laugh at it from a safe distance away.

The Benign-Violation Hypothesis argues that something is funny when it meets two conditions at the same time: first, the situation must be viewed as a breach of normality; it must violate the expectation of the status quo. Secondly, this violation must be perceived as benign; it must be evident that the violation in question will not actually cause harm. In a nutshell, the hypothesis states that "anything that is threatening to one's sense of how the world 'ought to be' will be humorous, as long as the threatening situation also seems benign." (McGraw 2010:2)

Consider the following two scenarios:

1. Before he passed away, Keith's father told his son to cremate his body. Then he told Keith to do whatever he wished with the remains. Keith decided to bury his dead father's ashes.

2. Before he passed away, Keith's father told his son to cremate his body. Then he told Keith to do whatever he wished with the remains. Keith decided to snort his dead father's ashes. (Ibid:3)

In the first scenario, nothing unexpected occurred. This is the 'control version' of the story. In the second scenario, however, the idea of Keith snorting a track of his father's ashes probably elicited some feelings of disgust, if not downright offence. According to the research of Peter McGraw and Caleb Warren, over eighty percent of people responded to this scenario by agreeing that this "behaviour is wrong".

At the same time, this very same scenario also makes almost forty percent of people laugh. It's wrong and it's funny, simultaneously.

As the benign violation theory goes, the ash-snorting scenario is humorous to some people first because it imagines a bizarre and offensive violation of cultural, moral, and social norms. But importantly, at the same time, the scenario is perfectly benign because, at the end of the day, no one is actually hurt or injured by Keith's behaviour. Therefore, we might think of humour as presenting us ideas about the world that are both 'wrong' and 'not wrong' at the same time.

Likewise, a joke or pun can also be thought of as a quirky violation of reality, but one that appears to be harmless just the same. A contradiction of what we expect, but a contradiction that turns out to be benign. When we realize that such a contradiction is harmless, our immediate reaction seems to be to laugh at it. Next time you are listening to a comedian, try listening for these benign violations.

If the benign violation hypothesis is valid, it demonstrates further evidence that our ability to anticipate and predict the world is an underlying cornerstone of human cognition. We move about the world primarily on the basis of what we predict it will do. When we are confronted by something we did not forecast -- when the world does not abide by our predictions -- we tend to lash out in anger or recoil in disgust. Truly, as far as we know, anything unpredicted might be dangerous. However, when the unpredicted turns out to be harmless... now, that's funny. And laughing, as the theory goes, is the signal that evolved to let others know that, "It's ok! You shouldn't worry!"

Humour depends on our predictive conjecture. Without having assumptions about the world to violate, there would not really be anything to laugh about. A good laugh is a gentle reminder that the world isn't necessarily everything you presumed it to be. Perhaps laughter is, in fact, a kind of cognitive therapy.

Stigma

Consider this scenario: a man with Tourette Syndrome is sitting on a crowded bus. Let us randomly select another passenger, and consider her response to his actions and vocalizations.

As far as she is concerned, her fellow bus passengers pose no threat to her, but only as long as they behave in the normal, predictable patterns known to commuters. Her awkwardness at his outbursts reflects her inability to formulate an informative, predictive framework for his next action. He fails to meet the criteria she has set for predictability. Unable to coherently anticipate his behaviour, she cannot envisage a response beyond her first, immediate inclination to fight or run away. Her natural response is thus, in a word, fear.

The woman arrives home. Later she is visited by a friend. Over a drink, her friend expresses feelings of sorrow and anxiety. "Sometimes," he sighs, "I really do not think there is any point to life at all. I'm not sure it's even worth living. I'm thinking about ending it all." The same response is triggered: even though her friend is no erratic stranger, the disclosure of his depression severely undermines her ability to predict his next move. She feels a crippling inability to effectively address the situation, not unlike what she experienced on the bus earlier that day.

When a man on a bus shouts seemingly random noises,
and when a friend confesses thoughts of suicide,
both individuals undermine her ability to sense their agency;
her ability to anticipate and relate to their intentions is thwarted.

When I cannot coherently make sense of what is going on in your mind, my instinctual reaction will be to either pre-emptively disarm your capacity to harm me (fight) or create as much distance as I can between us (flight). Either way, my reaction is a natural, prejudicial act of self-defence. Fear is my innate response. Any agent that cannot be understood cannot be trusted; an incoherent agent must be considered a threat before being proved otherwise.

This inclination to react against what we cannot predict, anticipate, relate to, and understand goes by another word: stigmatization.

Consider how we as a society are presently addressing prejudice towards individuals with neurological disorders (such as Tourette's) and mental health issues (such as depression). Many of our contemporary campaigns to eliminate stigma seem to implicitly assume that stigma and prejudice are unnatural and immoral. As a result, we find ourselves more or less guilted into accepting differences. But there might be a potential danger in this, since most of our attempts to eliminate stigma do not in fact address the root neurological mechanisms of bias -- our capacity of prediction, agency detection, and self-defence. Our glossy awareness campaigns and slogans promote a highly superficial notion of acceptance. Consequently, we are taught to socially suppress our natural reactions under a guise of political correctness.

I worry that stigma cannot be eliminated by moral fortitude. We are hard-wired to fear what we cannot understand. These are deeply seated reactions, and much more complicated than awareness campaign adverts let on. Therefore, denaturalizing and demonizing stigma are strategies with the potential to backfire in the long run. Addressing the root of stigma means, first, accepting it as a natural inclination. I will only become a less prejudiced person as I become more aware of my own unconscious need to identify threats and unpredictable agents: only then can I consciously accept as benign that which was previously awash in fear. I must understand the causations of my prejudices if I am to have any hope of actually eradicating them. Pretending to not be prejudiced helps no one.

As an individual, this journey must last for my entire lifetime, for the future is sure to bring along new people and situations who first naturally elicit my fearful instincts. It makes no sense to claim that I have righteously eliminated the curse of prejudice from my life once and for all. Far better, I believe, to embrace the 'curse' it is as an innate attribute of my own mental makeup.

Better to anticipate the signs of its arrival in my attitude than outrightly deny its latent presence.

They say the opposite of love is not hate, but fear.
Inasmuch as community is the presence of trust,
and trust is the absence of fear,
a society is only as strong as its members' willingness
to dissect their own fear of one another.

For then, and only then,
can the person who was once
unconsciously perceived to be a threat
be finally, fully, and consciously accepted
as an equal.

AFFECT MISATTRIBUTION

"Thank you for agreeing to participate in this study," says the researcher, as she ushers you into a computer lab. She pulls up a chair in front of a monitor and invites you to take a seat.

"The purpose of this study," she informs you, "is to better understand how people make simple but quick judgments. You do not happen to speak or read in Chinese, do you?"

"Uh, no. I do not understand Chinese," you respond.

"Ok. On this monitor you are going see a series of different images. Some images are of the current president, some images are of the candidate challenging in the next election, and some images are just grey squares. After each of these images is displayed on the screen, a Chinese pictograph will appear. Every time you see these Chinese character symbols, please enter how you feel about the pictograph by pressing one of these buttons: Pleasant, Neutral, or Unpleasant."

The researcher starts the program and leaves you to complete the survey. Immediately, a big message appears on the screen:

It is important to note that the real-life image can sometimes bias people's judgments of the drawings. Because we are interested in how people can avoid being biased, please try your absolute best not to let the real-life images bias your judgment of the drawings! Give us an honest assessment of the drawings, regardless of the images that precede them. (Payne, et al. 2005: 284)

Very well, you think to yourself, I am merely giving my reactions to the pictographs.

You spend several minutes completing the survey on the computer. Upon completion, you are given another questionnaire, which then specifically asks you how you feel about each political candidate and the degree to which you identify with their platforms, ideologies, and leadership competency. Your contribution to the research study is finally complete, but here things get interesting for the investigators.

As it turns out, a significant majority of your feelings towards the Chinese pictographs correlate with the images of the president and the opposing party candidate that you were shown before each symbol. Statistically speaking, the pictures that represent ideological beliefs influenced your reported opinions about random symbols that you have never seen before in your life. Remarkably, this occurred even though you were explicitly instructed not to let the images bias your responses.

You have just participated in an Affect Misattribution study. The pictures of the political candidates were "primes" that somehow informed your reactions to symbols that were otherwise meaningless to you. You might think about it this way: many people are repulsed by the image of a swastika because of its association with the Third Reich. But the swastika is not actually an invention of the Nazis, it can be found on historical artifacts spanning across cultures. Present day disgust towards the swastika occurs because of what the symbol now represents, not because there is something inherently repulsive in the particular arrangement of pixels that make up the symbol itself. Even though the swastika has become a morally-charged symbol over the course of many years, the affect misattribution hypothesis suggests a similar psychological phenomenon can occur in just milliseconds. (Ibid:291)

What you see in one moment elicits a reaction that frames the way you see the next moment. And so it goes, around and around. At no moment does your mind perceive the world without being informed by the previous moment. Like the individual frame of a movie, this second of life only makes any sense at all if it is appended to the last second.

Today, even though we might be reminded to consciously check our biases, we are no more able to stop subconsciously applying assumptions about the world onto what we see. Perhaps, then, our highest call is not to imagine ourselves free from bias, but rather to better comprehend how our biases reciprocally generate our ideas about life.

FRAMING EFFECT

Let's imagine that you are a high-ranking health official for your country. One day you are called into an emergency meeting. A deadly virus has been reported by several hospitals in another country. It is estimated that 600 people will die. There are two different strategic proposals being considered to mitigate the devastating impact of the virus for the citizens of your country:

If Program A is adopted, 200 will be saved.

If Program B is adopted, there is a 1/3 probably that 600 will be saved, and 2/3 probability that no one will be saved.

Which of the two programs would you favor? (Tversky & Kahneman, 1981:453)

A vote is taken. 72 percent of the room supports Program A, and only 22 percent are in favour of Program B. An almost three-quarter majority believes that Program A is the better option of the two.

Then one of your colleagues earnestly raises her voice. "Wait! You need to look at these numbers the other way." She explains the probabilities differently:

If Program A is adopted 400 people will die.

If Program B is adopted, there is a 1/3 probability that nobody will die, and a 2/3 probability that 600 will die.

This time, only 22 percent of the attendees support Program A, and 78 percent support program B. Simply by flipping the wording of the question, your perceptive colleague has swung the vote completely in the opposite direction. No matter how it is worded, the consequences and odds remain the same; the difference lies merely in whether they are stated in the positive or negative.

In psychology, this is known as the framing effect: we tend to avoid risk when a positive frame is presented and embrace risk when a negative frame is presented. In fact, it is altogether possible that some of the biggest risks we have taken in our own personal lives have been in response to negative frames.

After repeatedly demonstrating this pattern in human decision-making, psychologists Amos Tversky (1937-1996) and Daniel Kahneman (b. 1934) put forth a compelling question: are we really rational creatures when it comes to our choices? Rather than assuming that we actually make optimal choices in life, the psychologists proposed that we make decisions based on how we perceive the gains and losses involved -- not by rigorously analyzing the final outcomes that our decisions produce.

Today you may be faced with some options. Remember: the way you frame these options are just as important as the options themselves. Whether you tend to see the glass as half empty or as half full, experiment by looking at your options in the opposite way.

MAPS

The *Hereford mappamundi* is an ancient medieval map, dated circa 1285. It portrays Jerusalem at the centre of the world, and the Garden of Eden at the edge, protected by a wall of fire. Including religious and mythological symbolism on maps is virtually as old as mapmaking itself. In fact, one of the world's oldest known maps comes from Babylon, probably originating in the early sixth century BCE, and it includes cuneiform explaining the cosmic creation myth of the world; the epic battle between Ti'amat and Marduk.

As medieval maps tend to orientate themselves around Jerusalem, so too the Babylonian map places the city of Babylon at its centre. Similarly, the Kangnido map, created in 1470s Korea, geographically emphasizes the seat of imperial power. Every map was made for a purpose. Just as the map application on your phone automatically triangulates to your current location or global position coordinate, so too every map in the history of the world is created and utilized by agenda-driven human beings.

Every map reflects much more than a neutral description of the geography: cultures of mythology see the world symbolically, cultures of commerce focus on routes for trade, cultures of commercialism see the world in terms of retail opportunities. Nobody can 'just make' a map, because every map is an abstraction of the world. A map is a conditional distillation of space. Every mapmaker must make arbitrary decisions about what to include: which landmarks are valuable? where do people care about going? who decides which areas to include? who will read the map, and what is important to them? Since a map can never fully capture the world as it really is in an absolute sense, every map is just as much a proposal about the world as it is a reflection of it. (Brotton, 2012:438) Every map inherently celebrates something about the world and marginalizes something else about it.

Ultimately, a map allows us to see who we are in light of the whole. After all, what is the use of hanging a map of the world on the wall? It is not detailed enough to use for actual navigational purposes -- you never see a tourist walk through a geographically significant area consulting a world map as a guide! What is the meaning of a map that has such little applicability? Even when a map does not coherently demonstrate how to go somewhere, it speaks volumes about the attitude of its creators and owners and how their political, intellectual, or physical specificities relate to the planet.

Historians depend on maps as vital windows for understanding the perspectives of bygone civilizations. Today, however, it is easy for us to forget that the maps we use reflect an equal wealth of information about our contemporary attitudes and values. Perhaps it is because we think of our maps as 'absolute' pictures of the world that we do not recognize how many assumptions we leave embedded in them... and take for granted when using them.

PRAGMATISM

The American philosopher William James (1842-1910) suggested that there are primarily two modes (or 'temperaments') of thinking: rational thought and empirical thought.

Rationalism, as James describes it, "starts from wholes and universals" and explains the world on the basis of contemplation and logic. Rational truth is deduced through intellectual rigour. Empiricism, on the other hand, determines truth only by experience: sensory observation and evidence. Empiricism is concerned with what can be measured, tested, and proven. Opposite of rationalism, it "starts from the parts, and makes of the whole a collection." (James, 1907:10)

James believed that separating rational and empirical thought into isolated categories was incongruent to the actual experience of human life. "You find an empirical philosophy that is not religious enough, and a religious philosophy that is not empirical enough," he wrote. (Ibid p. 12) Human choice and reasoning is altogether too nuanced to simply categorize as two opposite modes. It would be extremely impractical for a person to live by pure empiricism or pure rationalism alone.

Therefore, James advocated a third option: pragmatism. He explained, "The term is derived from the same Greek word πρᾶγμα, meaning action, from which our words 'practice' and 'practical' come." (Ibid p. 26) Thus, pragmatism is a philosophy founded on a concern for practicality, consequence, and outcome of beliefs and ideas.

If we were to debate a great philosophical issue -- say, free will versus determinism, or materialism versus spirituality -- pragmatism would shift the focus from rationalism (logic and beliefs) and empiricism (experience and evidence) to a third question: why does this particular question even matter in the first place? Pragmatism is unapologetically utilitarian.

> What difference would it practically make to any one if this notion rather than that notion were true? If no practical difference whatever can be traced, then the alternatives mean practically the same thing, and all dispute is idle. Whenever a dispute is serious, we ought to be able to show some practical difference that must follow from one side or the other's being right. (Ibid pp. 25-26)

Importantly, James was not advocating that we abandon either rational or empirical thought. Rather, his emphasis was that our intellectual pursuits should be governed by their end goals and consequences. If this was our aim, rationality and empiricism could co-exist. At the heart of his argument: a person ought to be able to simultaneously adhere both to scientific objectivity on one hand and spiritual, theistic beliefs on the other. Neither set of beliefs, even though perhaps conflicting, ought to negate the other, because both answer to a higher commitment of practicality and consequence. In other words, what matters most is not just whether or not the belief is 'true' in either a rational or empirical sense, but what the belief means about the way you live and experience life.

> Rationalism sticks to logic and the empyrean. Empiricism sticks to the external senses. Pragmatism

is willing to do anything, to follow either logic or the senses and to count the humblest and most personal experiences. She will count mystical experiences if they have practical consequences... Her only test of probable truth is what works best in the way of leading us, what fits every part of life best and combines with the collectivity of experience's demands, nothing being omitted. (Ibid pp. 38-39)

As a philosophical mindset, James believed that pragmatism offered the best chance of discovering truth. It lifted the boundaries of both empiricism and rationalism.

[Empiricism] has in fact no prejudices whatsoever, no obstructive dogmas, no rigid canons of what shall count as proof. She is completely genial. She will entertain any hypothesis, she will consider any evidence. (Ibid)

Whereas empiricism says, "Truth is only that which I can test," and

rationalism says, "Truth is only that which I can reason in my mind,"

pragmatism asserts: "Truth shall be known only by its consequence."

Take the next twenty-four hours as a case study: are a majority of your efforts focused on proving your experiences are valid? Or perhaps proving that your beliefs are coherent? James might suggest that both of these pursuits are only exercises in self-validation. Rather than argue about the justification of your beliefs and experiences, he might turn the question around and ask: how have your beliefs and experiences predetermined your quest for truth? What are the consequences of your beliefs right now? How are you, and the world around you, any better or worse off for having been influenced by your idea of truth?

SQUIRREL

The American philosopher William James (1842-1910) told a story about a conversation he had on a camping trip. Upon arriving at the campsite after a solitary, leisurely stroll, he discovered his friends embroiled in an animated debate. The topic of their discussion: a squirrel. They explained the scenario: there is a squirrel clinging to the side of a tree trunk, while on the other side of the tree, a man is trying to catch a glimpse of the squirrel. As the man moves around the tree to see the squirrel, the squirrel moves around the tree, always remaining out of sight to the man on the opposite side of the tree trunk. The debate had become jovial uproar: as the man moves around the tree, does he actually move around the squirrel or not? (James, 1907, p. 25)

While James was away on his stroll, the comic dispute had become evenly split. Half the group argued that since the man was moving around the tree trunk he was obviously moving around the squirrel too, but the other group was adamant that since the tree always stood between the man and the squirrel, clearly the man was not moving around the squirrel. When James returned to the campsite, he was asked to weigh in on the matter.

The answer to the question, said James, depends entirely on the practical definition of 'going around' being used. If 'going around' means that the squirrel is in the centre of a compass, and that the man travels to the North, East, South, and West of the little critter, then yes, the man goes around the squirrel as he orbits the tree. On the other hand, if 'going around' means being in the front, right, back, and left of the squirrel, then no, the man does not go around the squirrel since the squirrel always keeps its belly towards the man. James argued technically both sides were right, and if they made the distinction as to what they meant by 'going around' then the argument would be settled.

The point of this seemingly trivial illustration was that disputes often stem from distinction errors and misunderstandings. For James, such disagreements are best met with this adage: "Whenever you meet a contradiction you must make a distinction." (Ibid) In this case, the distinction in question was the definition of 'to go around'. Focussing on who is right and who is wrong generally adds nothing to the dispute, for the more rigorous the debate, the more both sides confidently believe that coherent truth is on their side.

When it comes to settling disputes, helpful input is often less about joining the 'right' argument, but instead tracing the practical consequences of the discussion.

TOOLKIT

Imagine that your mind is a toolkit.

It is equipped with an impressive database of past experiences, memories, and easily accessible 'reaction modules'. Moment by moment, unconscious to your own awareness, you exercise this arsenal of knowledge: you stop at red lights, you shake hands or exchange appropriate social gestures, and you use cutlery, escalators, and refrigerators effortlessly, without needing to relearn their functions every time you encounter them.

You move through life with a high degree of confidence. You know the purpose, utility, and consequence for the objects and cultural norms in your field of existence. Your toolkit meets your needs well, freeing your mind for perceptive creativity and more complex problem-solving (instead of trying to figure out door handles, idioms, and TV remotes from conceptual scratch, day after day).

For this reason, although necessary, this toolkit can also be a liability. Whenever a new object, idea, or perception enters your mind, these automatic mechanisms will respond, using whatever past material they can find to interpret the present phenomenon. There is no such thing as an undefined perception or a neutral accounting for experience -- you have survived this long precisely because this mental framework instantaneously differentiates between danger and reward, fighting or flying, without waiting for your higher levels of consciousness to debate it.

As a consequence, everything that is new, strange, or unfamiliar to you today will be automatically processed. Long before you think that you are thinking rationally, a whole set of assumptions have already been established, leaving your self-supposed objectivity to be more illusionary than real. As William James said, "A great many people think they are thinking when they are merely rearranging their prejudices. (Quoted in Fadiman, 1955, p. 719) Or, in the words of David Bohm: "Normally our thoughts have us rather we having them." (Quoted in Senge, 2005, p. 29)

As a result, we live in a feedback loop of our reality interpretation. Once our toolkits establish a working model of the world, this model will self-defend against everything that might undermine or damage it. For example, a working model of existence that posits the presence of a creator or transcendent presence must naturally combat a contrary model which does not include divine forces, and vice versa. Both toolkits, or world views, are not merely defending a theoretical idea, but an entire system of self-referential organization that enables the individual to make sense of their existence.

> When a speculative philosopher believes he has comprehended the world once and for all in his system, he is deceiving himself; he has merely comprehended himself and then naively projected that view upon the world. (C.G. Jung, quoted in Shelburne, 1988, p. 40)

How then do we overcome the models of the world which our toolkits have constructed? Only through the will to question the answers -- even the most fundamental answers that we can imagine. The certainties which we take for granted become our primary objects of investigation. That which we know most intimately becomes the starting point for critique.

> There is an ever present readiness to abandon pursuit of critical thought in favor of a certainty which poses

as the answer, while it actually is the question. (Hacker, 1955, pp. 77-78)

If our worldview nullifies questioning, then we are, indeed, indefinitely, trapped in our own minds.

We are only able to discover as we are able to question our greatest certainties.

SATISFICE

Herbert Simon (1916-2001) was a highly influential American social scientist. He was very interested in the way people make decisions and solve problems. This led him to investigate a question that had been largely taken for granted, "How rational are humans, anyway?"

Pure rationality -- thinking through every dimension of a situation thoroughly -- requires two things that rarely, if ever, actually exist: an unlimited amount of time and an abundant surplus of cognitive resources. Therefore Simon argued that it is impossible to predict the behaviour of people as if they are thoroughly rational creatures. Rather, humans make decisions in a realm of "bounded rationality" that requires the construction of "a simplified model of the real situation in order to deal with it." (Simon 1957:199)

Put another way: when it comes to decision-making, people "adapt well enough to 'satisfice'; they do not, in general, 'optimize.'" (Simon, 1954:129)

The pressures of the real world enforce real constraints on the reach of objective, detached thought. We can only afford a limited infusion of mental energy into every decision and problem that comes along. Like everything, rationality is an expenditure -- it has a cost -- and more often than not, the price is higher than the payoff.

Enter: heuristics. This is a fancy word for the tools we use to make decisions as economically as possible. Heuristics are frugal reasoning methods: they enable us to reach conclusions quickly; they are mental shortcuts that waste as little time and energy as possible on the way to a decision. Heuristics include intuition, rules of thumb, common sense, and stereotyping.

Our heuristic strategies are built on our capacity to recognize patterns. The instantaneous decision to avoid a suspicious individual in an alley is based on recognizing a set of patterns that alerts you to the potential danger of the situation. Likewise, racism and stigmatization are highly heuristic: mental processes that apply patterns and assumptions about entire groups of people on to a single individual.

Amos Tversky and Daniel Kahneman point out that it is the "internal consistency of a pattern of inputs" that establish the degree of an individual's confidence in their heuristic judgments. (Tversky & Kahneman 1974:1126) For example, the images that come to mind when you hear the terms 'librarian', 'scientist', or 'Islamist' are simply the stereotypes you have generated by the application of pre-existing mental models. You conjure the notion of 'librarian' based on all the previous patterns of 'librarian' you have encountered. The phenomenon is complicated: on one hand, your conception of a 'librarian' is highly stereotyped. On the other hand, without the 'librarian patterns' that you apply to the concept, the word 'librarian' itself would be meaningless to you.

Heuristics are truly a double-edged sword. They enable us to effectively move around the world and interact within our societies. Without them, we could barely take a step without short-circuiting in neural overload. At the same time, heuristic patterning also creates seemingly impenetrable walls of bias and prejudice between individuals and entire ethnicities.

It is unlikely that we even have "access" to our heuristic toolkit: it is unconscious, buried deeply in our instinctual behaviour. It is inaccessible precisely because it enables us to make fast judgments, perceptions, and choices, without demanding higher cognitive resources.

However, today, perhaps we might seek to foster a greater awareness of the judgments that we make the most quickly: the less time we spend thinking about something, the greater our reliance on the patterns of previously acquired data. Do not simply review your decisions: review the patterns that inform your decisions.

BODY AND SOUL

AWESTRUCK

In all sensation, simple or complex, sharp or dull, the animal... feels that it lives. (Aristotle, On Sense and What is Sensed, 7.448a-448b)

When was the last time you were awestruck?

Researchers at Stanford argue that feelings of awe slow our perception of time. The sense that time is rushing by at a breakneck speed is dramatically 'offset' by moments of awe. The study suggests that being awestruck decreases our impatience and increases our tendency to help others. Awe heightens the value of lived experience above material acquisition, which suppresses the "time starved" feeling of nonstop activity. The researchers conclude by underscoring "the importance and promise of cultivating awe in everyday life." (Rudd et al 2012:1135)

Nicholas Humphrey theorizes that the purpose of consciousness is to be awestruck: our capacity to be enchanted by experience is our primary incentive to survive, and it compels us to keep surviving in spite of being cognizant of the fact we have a mortal expiry date. Perhaps there is, as Humphrey suggests, a "biological advantage to being awestruck." (Humphrey 2011:16) To live life is to appreciate it, and to appreciate life is to be conscious of it. Thus we are most conscious -- and most alive -- when we are in a state of awe. In this sense, we might say that awe fulfills the purposes for which we have consciousness.

From this perspective, the primal urge of consciousness is neither happiness nor pleasure, but rather the conscious mind seeks moments of dumbfounded speechlessness at the spectacle of being alive -- a spectacle that is so abundantly inspiring that it infuses us with the incentive to keep on living... and experiencing.

Novelist Milian Kundera writes that distilling all human existence into the Cartesian mantra, "I think, therefore I am," is a foolish exercise of intellectualism. Rather, he says, "I feel, therefore I am," applies to every living creature. (Kundera 1991:225) Consciousness is, first, the compulsion to feel.

Today, be awed by something. What does it mean for you, personally, to cultivate and nurture your sense of awe about life? After all, without an awe for life, life has little hope of being awesome at all.

EPITHELIUM

Look at your hand.

Like every other part of you, your skin is composed of cells. Epithelial cells, to be precise. These cells are so closely packed together that they form a waterproof, pathogen-blocking barrier between the inside of your body and the rest of the outside world. Your skin is simply, brilliantly, made up of millions of cells working together to keep the outside out and the inside in. And thankfully, for us, epithelial cells are extremely good at cooperating with one another towards this end.

The outermost layer of your skin (stratum corneum) is in a continual state of repair; epithelial cells are constantly dying and being replaced. For this to occur, the cells on the exterior of your body require nutrients, just like every cell inside you. On the interior, your epithelial cells adhere to a base membrane, which acts as an intermediate diffuser of nutrients from your bloodstream. This membrane also informs the epithelium 'network' of what it should secrete from the body.

Your skin, this remarkable cellular network, not only acts as the first barrier between you and the outside world, it also senses and perceives the outside world. Epithelial cells have nerve endings (neurons) that immediately share information with your nervous system -- when your hand touches your coffee cup, signals from the epithelial nerves are sent to the parietal lobe in your cerebral cortex, which in turn processes the experience of the cup's texture, temperature, and proximity.

From the standpoint of your cellular composition, it is remarkable to look at your hand and realize that you are simply staring at the exterior 'side' of an amazing 'epithelial blanket'. On the other side of this blanket, the rest of your organs and tissues work together to give you life -- but all those processes are encased by this tightly interlocking patchwork of cells.

Today, everything you touch is a remarkable phenomenon. Or, we should say: every experience is remarkable to the extent that we consciously allow ourselves to appreciate the complexity and brilliance of being alive.

Tabula Rasa

I think of a child's mind as a blank book. During the first years of his life, much will be written on the pages. The quality of that writing will affect his life profoundly. (Walt Disney, cited in Giroux & Pollock, 2010, p. 17)

The idea that every human brain begins as a blank slate (or, tabula rasa, in Latin) has been around for a long time. Aristotle likened the mind to "a writing tablet on which as yet nothing actually stands written." (Aristotle, On the Soul, III.4)

Ibn Sīnā (980-1037), the Persian thinker, believed that we are born only with an intellect, with nothing yet impressed upon it. We can imagine our state at the beginning of life, having "never heard an opinion, never believed in any doctrine, never associated with a religious community, and never known any government," but we experience all these things as "the objects of sense." (Ibn Sīnā, an-Najāt, cited in Gutas, 2012, p. 408)

Perhaps one of the most well known articulations of the tabula rasa idea comes from the English philosopher John Locke (1632-1704):

> Let us then suppose the mind to be, as we say white paper, void of all characters, without any ideas; how comes it to be furnished? Whence comes it by that vast store which the busy and boundless fancy of man has painted on it, with an almost endless variety? When has it all the materials of reason and knowledge? To this I answer in one word, from experience; in that all our knowledge is founded; and from that it ultimately derives itself. (Locke, 1836, p. 51)

Supposing that the mind begins as a blank slate incites the age old 'nature versus nurture' debate. If we do, in fact, start life as an empty sheet of paper, then who we become is largely the consequence of experiences. The nurture argument supposes that it is the ebb and flow of life (our experiences) that chisels our identity. We are essentially a reflection of the ideas, modes, and motifs that we have been exposed to. We only know what we learn along the way. This view is clearly expressed by Ashley Montagu as follows:

> With the exception of the instinctoid reactions in infants to sudden withdrawals of support and to sudden loud noises, the human being is entirely instinctless... Man is man because he has no instincts, because everything he is and has become he has learned... from his culture, from the man-made part of the environment, from other human beings. (Montagu, 1968, p. 11)

On the other hand, consider the arguments against the blank slate idea: neuroscience demonstrates that your brain is wired for fairly specific things, such as living in a social culture and using language. Being raised in either Asia or South America will hugely inform the kind of cultural behaviour you mimic and the specific language you use, but the important point here is that your brain's capacity for culture and language is innate -- built in to your neurological circuitry even before you started employing them. In fact, the only reason you could learn how to navigate a culture and express a language in the first place was because your brain came equipped to do so, 'out of the box' so to speak. In other words, maybe you did not start off life as 'blank' as you might have assumed. You did not simply scribble your cultural sensibilities and language skills on a tabula rasa -- it may have been more like filling out a form. You only learned these behaviours because your brain was essentially programmed with innate circuitry to begin with. (Pinker, 2004, p. 9) Your brain may not have been a blank slate as much as it was a protomap. (Mallamaci, 2011, p. 40)

To make this point, the French mathematician and philosopher Gottfried Leibniz (1646-1716) wrote a rebuttal to Locke's 'white paper' argument:

> The axiom handed down by philosophers: there is nothing in the mind that does not come from the senses, will be used as an objection to what I am saying. However, an exception has to be made of the soul and its affections: Nihil est in intellectu quod non fuerit in sensu; excipe: nisi ipse intellectus [There is nothing in the intellect that was not first in the senses, except the intellect itself]. (Leibniz, 1689, Book II, Chapter 1, §2)

The nature versus nurture discussion is famous for inciting strong emotional reactions. We often recoil against the idea of determinism -- many of us hate the suggestion that our so-called 'true essence' is more genetically preprogrammed than serendipitously discovered over a lifetime. As long as we believe that we are a mashup of what we are exposed to, we maintain a precious sense of self-determination for moving ahead. Along with Thomas Aquinas (1225-1274) we are inclined to believe that "the mind and intellect of man is of the very essence of the soul." (Aquinas, Summa Theologica, 79.2) Therefore, threats to the autonomy of the intellect are easily perceived to be threats to the soul. For many, questioning the autonomy of the mind means undermining our very sense of free will.

In spite of the centuries of debate and the tomes of philosophizing, the question of the tabula rasa can only be addressed by each of us in the present moment. Whether you consider your outlook on life to be the sum total of your experiences or the result of a neurological inheritance of genes, you will leave these words and, one way or another, decide what to do with the rest of your day. Whether through instinct or choice -- you still have to figure out what you are going to eat for lunch.

Perhaps the most practical and immediate implication of contemplating the tabula rasa comes as we consider our treatment of others. Whether the other people in our lives (spouse, children, coworkers, employers) are the products of their experience or products of their genetic lineage, we are confronted with the possibility that they are, like us, much more complicated than any single action might disclose.

Perhaps, in this respect, we might all seek to nurture an innate sense of thoughtfulness.

FLYING MAN

Ibn Sīnā (980-1037) was a Persian scientist and thinker. In the West, he is commonly known as Avicenna. Among his many contributions to medicine, science, philosophy, and physics, Avicenna also developed a framework for human psychology that would go on to influence many later thinkers.

One of Avicenna's most popular thought experiments goes like this: imagine yourself "falling in the air or the void" yet encountering no air resistance. For all practical purposes, you are suspended in a vacuum, neither touching nor being touched by anything. In fact, you do not even have a body at all: no limbs, "no internal organ, whether heart nor brain, and no external thing." (Marmura, 1986:387) You are, more or less, simply an immaterial element of consciousness dangling in space. You are aware that you exist, but you have no body and no physical contact with anything else.

For Avicenna, this thought experiment, which is popularly known today as the "Flying Man" argument, served as an "alerting and reminding" of the "existence of the soul". Since we can imagine the concept of existence without a body (and the concept of consciousness without a brain), then we must possess an immaterial soul (a fundamental 'I', or an inner 'self') that enables us to imagine such a state of existence in the first place. If we were purely and only physical creatures, how is it that our brains could even imagine ourselves apart from our bodies in the first place?

Self-awareness, then, is the first and most primal element of human cognition. And, since our self-awareness can be imagined apart from our physical bodies, then consciousness must be something that can live beyond the shells of our temporal, fleshly bodies too.

Skeptics of the "Flying Man" argument point out that Avicenna is assuming his point instead of proving it. He is not actually offering any evidence for the premise of a self-aware soul, but he is simply suggesting that our capacity to imagine the evidence is evidence enough.

Therefore, whether or not you buy Avicenna's idea of an immaterial soul, the "Flying Man" does, at the very least, highlight the spectacular capacity of the human imagination. For the sake of argument, let us assume that Avicenna is wrong and that we are, in fact, only physical creatures. In this case, the "Flying Man" is theoretically impossible because consciousness cannot exist apart from the brain and the body that supports it. Now, let us marvel at the capacity of this brain to theorize that the very consciousness that it gives rise to can exist apart from itself.

Here is the remarkable apex of human abstraction: our ability to imagine that we can exist apart from ourselves.

Soul or no soul, this ability is truly remarkable.

GHOST IN THE MACHINE

What is the soul?

> "soul"...refers to the innermost aspect of man, that which is of greatest value in him (Catechism of the Catholic Church, Article I. Paragraph 6. II.363)

The "irreligious deny the existence of God, and the distinctness of the human soul from the body," wrote Rene Descartes (1596-1650). For the French philosopher, belief in existence of God and the eternity of the soul were prerequisites for moral behaviour, since the irreligious are "restrained neither by the fear of God nor the expectation of another life." Thus, he argued, that the fact we have thinking, feeling, and reflecting minds is proof that we are more than our physical bodies alone:

> For when I consider the mind, or myself in so far as I am merely a thinking thing, I am unable to distinguish any parts within myself; I understand myself to be something quite single and complete....By contrast, there is no corporeal or extended thing that I can think of which in my thought I cannot easily divide into parts; and this very fact makes me understand that it is divisible. This one argument would be enough to show me that the mind is completely different from the body... (Descartes, 1984, Vol II, p. 59)

Descartes also framed the argument in another way: I have a distinct idea of myself as a thinking creature but, on the other hand, I also have a distinct understanding that parts of my body are non-thinking as well. "And accordingly," he reasoned, "it is certain that I am really distinct from my body, and can exist without it." (Ibid p. 54) In philosophical terms, this observation became known as Cartesian Dualism, the separation of the mind from the body.

But later philosophers would adamantly disagree. Gilbert Ryle described the division of the mind and the body as a self-made illusion: the "dogma of the Ghost in the Machine," as he called it. (Ryle, 1949, p. 22) This dogma, Ryle argued, was born because Descartes made a "category-mistake" about the nature of the mind. Descartes failed to accept that every part of our being -- from our metabolisms to our cardiovascular systems, and yes, our minds themselves -- operate in processes and cycles. All together, life is a symphony of coordinated subprocesses, not the least of which is the sensing and perceiving of mind. Subconsciously, the mind triggers fight or flight responses, cognitively processes stimuli, coordinates the nervous system, automates evasive manoeuvres, and so much more. "The representation of a person as ghost mysteriously ensconced in a machine" comes from failing to recognize the mind as an equally biological organ. (p. 18) For philosophers like Ryle, arbitrarily separating the mind from all the other interdependent components of a person is a counter-intuitive (and categorical) mistake.

But what happens to our conception of the human soul when we exorcise the ghost from the machine? Francis Crick, co-discoverer of DNA structure, described this as the "Astonishing Hypothesis" -- the proposition that every emotion, ambition, recollection, and even your most innate 'sense of self' is ultimately nothing more than a result of nerve cells and molecules. (Crick, 1994, p. 3) The holism of this hypothesis is all encompassing: everything that makes you "you" is encapsulated in your neurons, and nowhere else in the cosmos. You are not an avatar, incarnation, or embodiment of anything beyond your immediate organic composition. Moment to moment, no reality that you can experience is simultaneously inconsistent with the physiological activity of your brain.

As astonishing as this hypothesis may be, its advocates account increasing evidence in its favour: We know that severing the corpus callosum (that is, isolating the left and right hemispheres of the brain, which is an operation often performed for people suffering from epilepsy) can result in a disunity of conscious experience. (Bayne, 2008) We know that a stroke can eliminate a mental faculty, such as the appreciation of music, capacity for language, or even moral reasoning abilities. And we know that psychoactive drugs can profoundly affect behaviour, decision-making, and the fundamental experience of life itself. Increasingly it seems that Ryle was correct: the mind is not a ghost in the machine; the mind is inseparable from the machine. Or, perhaps more to the point, the mind is the means by which we define ourselves as machines. And a brilliant machine we are: a hundred billion neurons, interconnected by a hundred trillion synapses. To see the mind as a ghostless machine is not to devalue the complexity of human thought and behaviour. Nor does it devalue humanity. Perhaps it only goes to make the miracle of consciousness that much more spectacular.

For some, losing belief in the ghost equals a crisis of existential faith. Like Descartes, they fear that losing their soul simply turns conscious existence into a life sentence of nihilism.

Others celebrate the riddance of the ghost, decrying the notion of the soul as an artifact of ancient, untenable superstition. They embrace the hypothesis that the totality of consciousness resides only in the material stuff of our grey matter.

What do you believe about the ghost in the machine?

FREEWILL

...everything which becomes must of necessity become owing to some Cause; for without a cause it is impossible for anything to attain becoming. (Plato, Timaeus, 28a)

Of everything whatsoever a cause or reason must be assigned, either for its existence, or for its non-existence. (Spinoza, Ethics, I.14)

...nothing happens without a reason why it should be so rather than otherwise. (Leibniz, 2002[1715]:7)

Gottfried Leibniz coined it "the principle of sufficient reason" (ibid) and the idea itself is quite simple: nothing happens without something to cause it.

Intuitively, our lives are closely bound to this principle. Suppose that a piece of furniture around you spontaneously combusts and blows up into a million tiny shards. You would instantly assume there was a cause. Things do not just randomly explode without explanation.

That is evident enough.

But what about human choice? If every action has a causal impetus behind it, what determines your choices? The implications of the 'principle of sufficient reason' are enormous when you consider it in terms of human will.

Aristotle proposed this scenario: suppose a man is hungry and thirsty. He is sitting precisely between a plate of food on one side and a glass of water on the other. If his desire for food and drink is completely equal, and if the plate and the glass are exactly an equal distance away, Aristotle speculated that he is "bound to stay where he is," as if immobilized by the equilibrium of his desire. (Aristotle, De Caelo, II, 13.295b)

Of course, the idea that a man would starve or dehydrate while sitting between food and water -- unable to decide which to consume first -- seems rather ridiculous. So let's throttle back the intensity of the illustration: suppose you visit a restaurant this evening, peruse the menu, and realize you have an equal affinity for salmon and steak entrees. How do you choose between them?

If the principle of sufficient reason is true, then there must be an explanation for your selection, whether you are conscious of the reason or not. Perhaps you think to yourself, "Well, I had seafood last night, so I guess I'll have the steak tonight" or "The salmon dish is a couple of bucks cheaper, so I'll go with that one." In this case, as with most decisions you make, you are highly cognizant of the reasons that have shaped, influenced, weighed, and determined your choice.

But what if you do not have a reason to choose one instead of the other? What if you just pick a menu item at random because you cannot decide?

If the principle of sufficient reason is true, random does not exist. In other words: your menu selection must be caused by something. Even if you tape the menu to a wall and throw a dart at it (with the intent to purchase whichever entree is randomly impaled by the projectile) the causes of your final decision are nonetheless evident: your muscle strength, the angle and velocity of throw, and so on (not to mention your proclivity for making decisions by throwing things).

Eradicating randomness from the universe seems like a terrifying proposition; if we apply the principle of sufficient reason to account for everything, even every signal that passes through my brain is potentially beyond my control. Taken to its logical consequence, every concept and idea that "just seems to come to me" from the mysterious realm of the imagination is theoretically explainable by some material, precipitating cause. If every passion, every desire, every hope -- everything in me -- is caused by something, then how could I really assume that I have a free and autonomous and independent will?

If everything happens as the result of a reciprocal series of actions and reactions, then is my sense of freewill just a delusion?

On the other hand, if Leibniz's principle of sufficient reason is universally true, then everything about who I am today and the situation that I presently find myself in, is rooted in causations that are specific, determining, and maybe even explainable. In this version of the world, there are no accidents, only consequences. If this is the case, then perhaps one of the most important events that can happen in my lifetime is an epiphany: I am not actually making choices like a free agent in the universe, but I am being shaped and sculpted by existence itself, and this leads to an incredible possibility: existence is being shaped and sculpted by me in return.

Today, I am no less a maker of my world than a consequence of it. What, then, shall I choose to do with this opportunity?

THE EVOLUTION OF BELIEF

As long as my knowledge works satisfactorily, I am generally ready to suspend doubts about it. (Berger, 1966, p. 44)

Premise: Right now, in this moment, you and I are both convinced that our beliefs about the world are closer to reality than they have ever been in our lives up to this point. Hitherto, every belief that we have rejected along the way has been replaced by a new belief. Our current beliefs are the sum of our understanding thus far. And, as far as we can tell, our present beliefs about the world are as close to reality as we can get -- if we thought otherwise, we would have already changed our beliefs before now. You, me, and every person we meet, lives by the guiding assumption that our perceptions of the world are true to reality, or at least as true as they could possibly be by now. False and misguided beliefs -- at least the ones we have become aware of -- have already been reconfigured.

> The conclusion is tautological but inescapable: one believes what one believes, and one does so without reservation... If one believes what one believes, then one believes that what one believes is true, and conversely, one believes that what one doesn't believe is not true, even if that is something one believed a moment ago. We can't help thinking that our present views are sounder than those we used to have or those professed by others. (Fish, 1980, p. 361)

Simply, "there is never a moment when one believes nothing..." (Ibid p. 319) From this premise, Stanley Fish argues that relativism is technically an impossible position to hold. For instance, I cannot say, "All beliefs are equally valid" because this position would require me to believe that my own beliefs now are no truer to reality than any other belief. If this is the case, I have no reason to believe that "All beliefs are equally valid" is any more correct than the opposite position that "Only one belief is valid."

In other words, according to Fish, if I believe that relativism is true, I am no longer a proper relativist.

> No one can be a relativist, because no one can achieve the distance from his own beliefs and assumptions which would result in their being no more authoritative for him than the beliefs and assumptions held by others, or, for that matter, the beliefs and assumptions he himself used to hold. (Fish, 1980, p. 319)

Beliefs are evolving entities. However, in terms of day to day living, they feel concrete since they must provide us a framework to behave and make decisions. Fish's argument: no matter what we believe (including the relativist, skeptic, and solipsist) our beliefs serve as our orientation to (and description of) reality. Inasmuch as we all perceive the world, we are all inwardly clinging to something which we declare to be 'the truth'.

> This does not mean that one is always a prisoner of his present perspective. It is always possible to entertain beliefs and opinions other than one's own; but that is precisely how they will be seen, as beliefs and opinions other than one's one, and therefore as beliefs and opinions that are false, or mistaken, or partial, or immature, or absurd. That is why revolution in one's beliefs will always feel like progress, even though, from the outside, it will have the appearance merely of change. (Ibid p. 361)

Perhaps one of the most amazing traits of human beings is that our beliefs even change at all. Remarkably, over the years of a life, one's perspective and ideas can slowly shift a hundred and eighty degrees. But the change is not usually linear: our beliefs are a beautifully convoluted patchwork of adjustments, compensations, tentative guesses, and, sometimes, simple nonsense that we just cannot let go of. In total, the changes make us who we are, a pastiche of beliefs.

Today, your beliefs will make your world and, at the same time, they might even evolve themselves.

CROISSANT

Let's pretend that your brain is a croissant roll. (Atran, 2002:42)

The crusty exterior, which is only about three millimetres thick, is your cerebral cortex. But what's inside, you ask? Well, tear the croissant apart down the middle and take a look.

The interior of the croissant is like a microscopic network of little bread fibres, weaving their way around and through small pockets of air. (These air pockets were created by carbon dioxide, as the yeast converted the glucose in the flour during a chemical process that caused the dough to rise prior to baking.)

The next time you enjoy a croissant or a slice of bread, look closely at the internal patchwork of tiny 'strings' that compose the loaf. Notice how bread is interconnected: thousands of little routes and veins that overlap and intersect to connect all the parts of the croissant.

Now consider the interior of your brain, which is composed of billions and billions of tiny little nerve cells (neurons). Connecting from the 'hub' (soma) of each neuron is an array of tiny little input 'strings' (dendrite) that receives electrochemical signals before sending them out (via axon 'strings') to other neurons.

As demonstrated by our croissant, one of the most fascinating characteristics of the brain is its interconnectivity. Just as each part of the croissant is attached to itself through millions of different connections, likewise your neurons can route processing signals through a seemingly infinite number of channels. The brain works exponentially, not linearly. Just try counting the number of potential 'crumb pathways' from one side of the croissant to the other... your brain is intertwined and cross-referenced to such a higher degree that you can barely use your brain to imagine it.

Picture what is happening in your brain at this 'systems level' when you listen to a comedic monologue, or type an email, or prepare a meal, or take a nice long stretch as you flop on the couch at the end of the day. All day, every day, your brain uses about twenty percent of your resting metabolic capacity. It is continually processing input and stimuli, translating everything into thought and behaviour. (Jabr, 2012)

Everything from your appreciation of music to your ability to recognize a friend's face arises as a result of this symphony of little neurons, endlessly and immeasurably interconnected with one another.

To be alive does not necessarily mean you are conscious of this astounding interconnectivity.

But it is this interconnectivity that allows you to be conscious of life.

You are these connections.

THE BURNING BUSH

And the angel of the Lord appeared unto him in a flame of fire out of the midst of a bush: and he looked, and, behold, the bush burned with fire, and the bush was not consumed.

And Moses said, I will now turn aside, and see this great sight, why the bush is not burnt.

And when the Lord saw that he turned aside to see, God called unto him out of the midst of the bush, and said, Moses, Moses. And he said, Here am I.

And he said, Draw not nigh hither: put off thy shoes from off thy feet, for the place whereon thou standest is holy ground. (Exodus 3:2-5, King James Version)

The supernatural is, by definition, counterintuitive and counterfactual.

When a fiery bush speaks to us, it disintegrates our categories: vegetation becomes animated by a force that gives it human-like agency and the dazzling capacity for a verbal exchange. The burning bush is supernatural precisely because the properties inherent to all other bushes -- namely, their lack of language -- are instantly undermined.

Because there is no reason to expect foliage to speak, an encounter with a talking bush is counterintuitive to the common experience of plant life.

Thus supernatural is counterintuitive in the sense that it thwarts all the metrics we use to measure existence on a daily basis.

Every supernatural event and ritual is an infusion and collision of disparate categories: a wafer of bread becomes a body; a finite human being receives a message from the infinite; a deceased organism is miraculously reborn.

A talking bush is also counterfactual because it violates our encyclopedic definition of vegetation. If talking bushes were a factual part of life, then a single talking bush would be no big deal at all. It is the counterfactual quality of a talking bush that makes it a supernatural occurrence. Counterfactual experiences propel us from the monotony of predictability by rewriting the rules of engagement with reality.

Thus, it is in the anomalous and amazing that we discover the supernatural. David Hume wrote:

> ...the more regular and uniform, that is, the more perfect nature appears, the more is he familiarized to it, and the less inclined to scrutinize and examine it. A monstrous birth excites his curiosity, and is deemed a prodigy. It alarms him from its novelty;

and immediately sets him a trembling, and sacrificing, and praying. (Hume 1889[1757])

Across continents, cultures, and history, one thing is evident: we, the human clan, cherish many beliefs that are patently contrary to the physical world of facts and intuition. No matter where you go in the world, you will find individuals who believe that some particular revelation, prophecy, or scripture lifts the veil on the natural world, exposing an invisible domain that animates all existence, and revealing a layer of reality that lays hidden just below the surface of everyday 'truths' as we know them.

Evidentially, the supernatural runs deep in our psychology: When our beliefs are confronted with contrary evidence, we reinforce our passion and commitment to them. (Bateson, 1975) When we hear stories that include counterintuitive elements we tend to remember them longer and retell them better than mere factual stories. (Atran, 2002) Our brains naturally respond to spiritual experiences, meditation, worship, and practices of committed belief. (Newberg, 2009)

In short, our beliefs in the counterintuitive and counterfactual is a trademark of our species.

We seem desperate to explore a domain beyond the measurable substrate of physical matter. Our attention is helplessly arrested by stories and mythologies that blatantly contradict the laws of nature that we otherwise depend on. Perhaps it is for this reason that we are predisposed to the supernatural, as if addicted to capturing events that live beyond the reach of everyday intuition and fact checking. We long to see the world not as it immediately presents itself, but as it might be. To be human is to worship the potentiality of the universe.

Those of us who believe in talking bushes do not stand aghast when we are told that such beliefs are counterfactual. Rather, the fact that the belief is counterfactual is likely what inspired the commitment of our belief in the first place. Thus, belief does not recoil in an absence of facts, because it was born in the absence of facts. Supernatural beliefs cannot be proven wrong due to their glaring lack of empirical confirmation, for their being superior to nature means that the nature can neither validate nor disprove them. As a species, little else seems to excite us more than this superiority: to understand humanity is to appreciate our propensity to be mesmerized by the spectacle of the impossible. We are lured by the impossible. We deceive one another with the impossible. We marvel at the impossible.

LIFE

COLLECTIVE

ANOTHER ME

Donald Brown (b. 1954), an American anthropologist, rented a house in the capital city of Brunei while doing research on the peoples and cultures of Southeast Asia. One day he found himself sitting on a wooden bench in front of the house, accompanied by a few young men from the community. After a while, Brown grew uncomfortable sitting on the bench and decided to sit on the walkway instead. As he changed locations, the rest of the men did likewise.

In Brunei culture it is uncouth to sit on a surface that is higher than another person unless, of course, you outrank them. Brown insisted that the Brunei men could remain seated on the bench but they insisted that such behaviour would not be appropriate. After all, they explained, what if other people saw us being so disrespectful to a visitor?

Brown often retold this story to his university students, using it as an illustration of the difference between the two cultures. He notes that anthropology has been largely built on investigating the multitude of dissimilarities and contrasts between ways of human life across the planet. One of the most fascinating aspects of ethnography is discovering how cultural phenomena are so vast and varied.

However, as he continued his research, Brown began to see this story in a completely different light. Instead of focusing on the dissimilarities between Brunei and American culture, he realized that instead, the story actually highlights more cultural commonalities: concern for the opinions of others, clear rules for determining politeness, a clear conception of rank (symbolized by highness and lowness), etc. In other words, the so-called 'cultural differences' were more like slight variations on a base of commonly shared categories. (Brown, 1991:1-2)

Brown's program of research evolved into an investigation of human universals: which traits, characteristics, and behaviours are shared by every person and culture in the world? Rather than dissecting the broad variance of human culture, what features are identical in every single person's experience of existence?

Is it even possible to compile a comprehensive list of human commonalities? Linguistic similarities alone are numerous: phonemes, grammatical structures, metaphor, and context specific standards (such as poetry and rhetoric) are present in every culture. Languages themselves vary greatly, but the baseline mechanism of language itself seems to be universally hardwired. Likewise are traits like facial recognition, kinship categories, tool-making, shelter construction, communicative gestures, musical composition, childbirth preparations, group identification, markers of social prestige and hierarchy, divisions of labour, adolescent rites of passage, demonstrations of hospitality and etiquette, norms of sexual modesty, mourning of death... the list is quite extensive. (Ibid 130-141)

On a personal level, human universals often appear as cultural differences because we rarely see how our own daily lives are manifestations of the very same global behaviours. For example, Westerners might not recognize that acquiring a driver's license stands as a normative rite of passage in a teenager's relationship to their society, nor how going to a cinema to enjoy a mythological narrative in digital surround sound manifests the universal practice of storytelling that resides in every culture.

We are rather predisposed to emphasizing our defining characteristics as a culture. When we look at other cultures, the first things we tend to see are the differences. (Perhaps comparing 'my culture' to the rest of the world is also a universal human trait.) But when we examine these differences closely, we discover that they are more like minor adaptations to a common human archetype.

Cultural variance is part of what makes Earth a spectacular array of human expression. The point here is not to pretend that we are all somehow identical to one another. To be sure, understanding a foreign culture can be as difficult as understanding its language. But the universality of these global, cultural denominators ought to remind us that 'the other' is also another 'me'.

Across the globe, we can discover how much we have in common by recognizing that our cultural differences are simply unique manifestations of our shared and universal human condition.

SOCIAL CAPITAL

A fool, said Thomas Hobbes (1588-1679), is a person who says in his heart, "there is no such thing as justice." (Leviathan 15.4) Such a fool simply cannot be trusted. Suppose you are going to trade favours with such a person; perhaps your foolish friend needs help moving to a new apartment at the end of the week, and you know you need to move at the end of the month. You help them move, but they do not reciprocate on your moving day. They have no reason to help. They have already received the help they needed -- why ought they expend themselves on your behalf now?

If you know this person is untrustworthy in advance, why would you bother to help them move in the first place?

David Hume (1711-1776), the Scottish philosopher, used an illustration of two farmers to highlight this dilemma:

Your corn is ripe today; mine will be so tomorrow. 'Tis profitable for us both that I shou'd labour with you today, and that you shou'd aid me tomorrow. I have no kindness for you, and know that you have as little for me. I will not, therefore, take any pains on your account; and should I labour with you on my account, I know I shou'd be disappointed, and that I shou'd in vain depend upon your gratitude. Here then I leave you to labour alone: You treat me in the same manner. The seasons change; and both of us lose our harvests for want of mutual confidence and security. (Hume, Treatise, III.2.5)

Obviously, both farmers would be better off if they cooperated with one another. Instead of losing portions of their crops, a partnership would drastically increase the likelihood that both harvests would be more successful. But, as it stands, they simply cannot trust one another.

Hobbes believed such deadlocks are solved by social contracts. Fools who break covenants or renege on their obligations to reciprocate inflict dire social consequences on themselves. They become the outcasts of a society and end up with the least social mobility. Hume, also, emphasized the importance of reputation. Both farmers must realize the social cost of not holding up one end of the bargain: the farmer who fails to reciprocate "subjects himself to the penalty of never being trusted again..."

Hence I learn to do a service to another, without bearing him any real kindness; because I foresee, that he will return my service, in expectation of another of the same kind, and in order to maintain the same correspondence of good offices with me or with others. And accordingly, after I have serv'd him, and he is in possession of the advantage arising from my action, he is induc'd to perform his part, as foreseeing the consequences of his refusal. (Ibid)

In contemporary verbiage, this stock of personal reputation might be described as 'social capital'. Like physical capital or human capital, social capital refers to the goodwill and trust that you leverage in your community. Social capital, like trust itself, is accumulated and built up over time. And it is acquired only by investment in others. Of course, social capital is impossible to measure in strictly empirical terms, but we seem to associate high levels of social capital with the strength of an individual's relational network and their willingness to cooperate with others for mutual benefit. Why would you choose to trust one person more than another? It is probably because they have earned your trust one way or another.

Taking it a step further, some social theorists like Robert Putnam suggest that high levels of social capital are correlated with increased levels of economic development. Stronger trust networks between people mean lower transaction costs and faster information sharing. In other words, the more social cohesion and trust between Hume's farmers, the more likely they are to coordinate a bumper harvest of corn. Putnam argues that the road to economic recovery today actually starts with community development: fostering neighbourhood associations, sports leagues, charitable organizations, and all sorts of endeavours that, on the surface, do not actually appear to be related to economics or politics at all. (Putnam, 1993)

This observation may be so simple and obvious that we are apt to gloss over it, but it warrants explicit reminders nonetheless: the more humans trust one another, the stronger, healthier, and more resilient their communities (and, by consequence, their societies as a whole) tend to become.

MICROBIOME

You are about ten percent human.

That is, for each cell that is genetically intrinsic to you, there are about ten other microbes -- bacteria, fungi, viruses, protozoal, etc -- living in symbiotic relationships with 'you' and with one another. They are on your skin, in your mouth, and especially concentrated in your gut -- where over forty million unique species alone are estimated to exist. (Turnbaugh 2007:805) In sum, you are the 'host' of about ten trillion bacteria.

All together, this massive community of microorganisms is known as your 'microbiota'. In your gut, bacteria break down certain foods that would otherwise be indigestible. By filling in every available space, they establish a natural defence system against pathogens. In your mouth, colonies of microbes compete for nutrition -- about a hundred million bacteria per millilitre of saliva. Without your bacteria, you would be limited to a very restrictive diet and be extremely susceptible to infections and disease. They educate your immune system -- which would be essentially worthless without them.

Under the microscope, we discover that our bodies host a dazzling array of life forms. Bacteria come in wildly different shapes: cocci are spherical; bacilli are rod-shaped; spirilla twist in a spiral. Some propel themselves by their flagella, some pull themselves along with small appendages, others twist and rotate. Of course, none of them have a brain, but all of them have a genetic lineage, and all of them have a mission.

So you might very well want to think of yourself as a superorganism. Strictly speaking, you are not composed of one species, but of millions. In fact, your microbiota accounts for far more genetic coding than your own genome. When you account for all these microbial genetics, the whole system is known as your 'microbiome' or, as some call it, your 'second genome'.

Microbes, like bacteria, have been around long before humans walked the earth. We have evolved together. We're in this together now. It is virtually impossible to theorize the existence of complex creatures (like ourselves) apart from this microbial world. Some researchers explain the human body as the microcosm of a rain forest: an ecological system of interdependent life forms, none of which could survive without the other. (Lozupone, 2012) Just as the planet sustains our lives, so too our bodies seem to be optimized for sustaining microbial life. (Pollan, 2013)

Life, wherever you find it, is the consequence of reciprocal and symbiotic relationships. In terms of microbiology, the answer to the question, "What is the meaning of life?" is an easy, evident reply: "To do your part." Survival, and thriving, is inseparable from supporting that which supports you.

QUORUM SENSING

Imagine yourself as a single-cell bacterium. You are happily living in your colony until one day, for reasons far beyond anyone's control, your community's reserve of nutrients is depleted. Your search for sustenance turns futile and now, it seems, the end is neigh.

Now, as a bacterium, you have two options for responding to this dire situation: sporulation or competence.

Sporulation essentially means choosing death. But before you perish you replicate your genome, wrap it in a membrane, and leave it behind as a genetic copy of yourself that can germinate again later when conditions are more favourable. By entering this dormant condition you embrace your demise, but your genetic code is left behind. As a spore, your DNA is almost indestructible: it is even able to withstand the solar electromagnetic radiation of outer space. (Horneck 1994)

Competence is your other option. All around you, millions of fellow bacteria are sporulating, and when they perish they leave behind their original genetic nucleotides, after encasing their new copied DNA in a spore. You are now surrounded by a supply of nutrients and bits of genetic code that could be very valuable to you. So maybe you should hold off on sporulating? But what if everyone else was to stop sporulating too? Then you would be in real trouble because it means you may have missed your opportunity to sporulate when you had the chance.

So how do you decide what to do? Well, in the absence of actually having a brain, you will not spend too much time fretting over the options. Rather, you are genetically wired to make this decision in concert with the rest of the colony. On a regular interval, you and every other bacterium emit a chemical signal expressing your current level of stress. Through this massive exchange of information, everyone knows the collective stress level of the community. This information is routinely processed by your genetic circuitry, as if by an interval timer. If stress levels are high enough, a random switch is thrown, determining whether or not you will sporulate. In other words, the signals you receive from your community set the threshold for your own 'decision'. Your decision, in turn, affects the threshold for the decisions of other cells. In this way, you are part of a massive self-regulating process. You are part of assuring adequate sporulation for future colonization, as well as calculating precise resource requirements of the present. (Schultz, et al, 2013)

Bacteria are living proof that the most expansive, adaptive, resilient, and successful forms of life are those that make collective 'decisions' to determine the needs of the present in light of the future. As a rudimentary form of life, and the most abundant kind of life on Earth, bacteria represent something fundamental about the nature of life itself.

Bacteria do not even have a cellular nucleus, but they are extremely self-organized nonetheless. Their 'decision-making process' is a huge enterprise of quorum sensing. There is no such thing as an isolated choice when it comes to making decisions about the future of your colony. Every choice is influenced by every other choice -- and every choice influences every other choice in turn.

There is little reason to think that the choices we make about our future, today, are any less consequential in the lives of those around us.

MEMES

Life is replication. Every living thing owes every ounce of its existence to some progenitor gene that made a copy of itself. It is towards this aim that every cell strives and it is the impetus of every living organism to reproduce. Life exists to make more life. Life that does not replicate ceases to exist.

In 1976, evolutionary biologist Richard Dawkins (b. 1941) made an observation: ideas seem to replicate like genes. In fact, culture itself is like a bunch of ideas that adapt and evolve over time as ideas are copied and produced. The only reason that any ideas or concepts find themselves passed from one generation to another is because they are copied from one generation to another.

Borrowing from the Latin word *mimeme* (imitation) and the French *mime* (memory), Dawkins coined the word meme to describe "a unit of cultural transmission" that is passed on by replication. Memes are like the operating system of a culture: everything from language and fashion to architecture can thus be imagined like modular packets of data, and each generation in turn replicates the ideas of the past. Like genetic replication, memetic duplication causes alterations that either help the idea spread or diminish its replicability in its particular environment. Thus, if you share a thought, idea, or song with me, it becomes like a parasitic propagation of the contagion from your mind to mine. (Dawkins, 1976, p. 192)

As the speed of telecommunication grew exponentially, so too did the speed at which memes could "go viral". As if almost proving the concept, the idea of memes itself became a meme — a cultural-linguistic concept that spread to virtually every person's mind.

Taking the idea even further, the psychologist Susan Blackmore thinks of the human mind as a memeplex — the core of our identity. This memeplex is like a synergetic interaction of all the memes we have acquired. It is here that all of our cultural ideas and norms, all together, define who we are as individuals. (Blackmore, 1999, p. 231) In other words, while your biological self is a construct of genes, your mental self is a composition of memes. Put a few people around a table sharing a coffee and conversation, and now you have a memeplex of memeplexes.

However, the world of memes isn't quite like the world of genes. The biggest problem of memes as a scientific hypothesis is a rather simple dilemma: what counts as a meme? How do you measure it? A strand of DNA has a beginning, middle, and an end, and it has very specific markers that define its parameters. Ideas, on the other hand, have very elusive boundaries. Cultural ideas blur, overlap, and intersect with one another indefinitely. Where does one idea end and another begin? If a meme is supposedly a genetic-like, self-contained module of data, how can it ever be measured and defined? (Atran, 2002, p. 241)

Furthermore, genes replicate with an extremely high rate of fidelity. Too much mutation or genetic drift and heredity information can be lost with great consequence. Ideas, on the other hand, merge and cross and reinvent themselves so quickly that there is no way to actually measure or identify a particular "species" of memes. Some of the biggest Internet memes, for instance, are radical abstractions and parodies of other memes. All we can do is infer the degree of influence that ideas have upon one another. Human ideas are not unlike the telephone game: the message is invariably altered by the time it goes around the circle of transmission. Genes, on the other hand, do much better at direct reproduction, or, more accurately, their duplication is just not as complex and creative as the network of human neurons that reproduce ideas.

Even though memes, at this point, seem more abstract than measurable, they do provide the material for a compelling thought experiment. Everything you hear, see, and speak today is your contribution to the memeplex of your community, workplace, or social environment. And one thing is certain: no meme-processing is neutral. The output is never quite identical to the input. The memetic universe is interesting precisely because every memeplex -- every human mind -- contributes just a slightly different description of it.

Two Thirds

It is 1981 and Alain Ledoux is a magazine editor. His periodical, *Jeux et Stratégie*, is devoted to strategy games and mathematical puzzles. He has a dilemma: the magazine is nearing the end of a massive reader competition and there are 4,078 contest participants in a tie for first place. Ledoux needs to determine a winner in a playoff round, so he presents a "psycho-statistique" puzzle: each reader must pick a number within a specific range, the winner being the number closest to two thirds of the average guess. (Sadrieh 2010:117)

For the sake of demonstration, suppose we were to replicate this contest: imagine that you, along with every other reader, is invited to submit an integer between 1 and 100. Your goal: guess what one third of the average guess will be.

Right off the bat, you probably realize that any guess above 67 is impossible, so you eliminate these impossible high numbers. Now, what is two-thirds of 67? Obviously, 45. But wait: if your fellow contestants were, like you, smart enough to figure out that the number could be no higher than 67, then they must also be smart enough to figure out that 45 is the optimal guess. Assuming they figured this out, you think to yourself, what is two-thirds of 45? Now you are down to 30. The logical degeneration continues until, finally, you arrive at 1.

Now, like Ledoux's readers, the question for you is not so much about what is mathematically logical, rather the question is this: how will you bet that other players will behave? To determine this, you not only ask, 'How smart are the other players?' but also, 'How smart do the other players think the other players are?' Your final guess will be a wager on what you think other people are thinking about other people!

What, then, defines a rational guess? Guessing 1 is logical. But guessing 1 may be an irrational guess if you assume that people will not follow the same logical sequence that you did. Depending on what you believe about the other contestants, a rational guess may be a mathematically irrational number.

This game demonstrates an observation described by British economist John Keynes (1883-1946) when he wrote,

> professional investment may be likened to those newspaper competitions in which the competitors have to pick out the six prettiest faces from a hundred photographs, the prize being awarded to the competitor whose choice most nearly corresponds to the average preferences of the competitors as a whole; so that each competitor has to pick, not those faces which he himself finds prettiest, but those which he thinks likeliest to catch the fancy of the other competitors, all of whom are looking at the problem from the same point of view. It is not a case of choosing those which, to the best of one's

judgment, are really the prettiest, nor even those which average opinion genuinely thinks the prettiest. We have reached the third degree where we devote our intelligences to anticipating what average opinion expects the average opinion to be. And there are some, I believe, who practise the fourth, fifth and higher degrees. (Keynes 1936)

Like free market investment, we might also describe our strategy for the number-guessing contest as "anticipating what the average opinion expects the average opinion to be." The "higher degrees" of analysis seek to account not just for other people's strategies, but also for the factors that influence their strategies, and then for the influences of those influential factors. Speculating about the speculations of other people opens up a kind of infinite regression... speculation on speculation about speculation!

But whether we're guessing in a number game or investing in the stock market, one thing is quite certain: we can never be quite certain what we are all going to do collectively until we actually do it. Today is a little bit like the number guessing game. Whether we're voting in an election, supporting a motion in a committee meeting, sharing a link on social media, deciding whether or not to join a revolution, or simply trying to avoid traffic jams, an underlying concern remains constant: what are other people's assumptions about the assumptions of others?

PACEMAKER

If you are reading this, the odds are very good that your heart is beating. The vital importance of that subtle, involuntary rhythm can be easily discovered by holding your breath for a few moments: an invasive discomfort that quickly becomes an impending sense of doom quickly spreads throughout your whole body. In only mere seconds you physiologically react to the muted supply of oxygen. Since every single cell that composes your body depends on oxygen, every single part of your body depends on the heart to circulate oxygen. If your heart stops beating, your cells -- and therefore, you -- suffocate.

Let's imagine that we were to perform a surgery: we open up your chest and extract some cells from the sinoatrial node (a tissue located in the right atrium of your heart). We place the cells in a Petri dish and examine them under a microscope. Amazingly, we would see that cells within an adequate proximity to one another will electrically pulsate together in unison. (Soen et al 1999) These specialized pacemaker cells have one single purpose: to coordinate a rhythm. In your body, their cues come largely from your nervous system, which indicates the oxygen supply needed throughout the whole organism, but even in a Petri dish their sole ambition to syncopate a little electrical charge remains the same. Again and again they electrically depolarize, causing a contraction. Right now, even as you read this, their little pulses signal the beat that is giving you life itself.

What does it mean to be alive right now? If you were to ask a sinoatrial node cell, its answer would be simple and immediate: coordinate with the pattern. If you ask a human, a complex of uniquely purposed cells, you obviously will get a much more unique and complicated answer.

In an interview about his 1964 novel Herzog, the writer Saul Bellow (1915-2005) said that "Many people feel a 'private life' to be an affliction. In some sense it is a genuine affliction; it cuts one off from a common life." Individualism, he thought, becomes "the imprisonment of the individual in a shameful and impotent privacy." As a person spends more and more energy trying to discern and discover his own 'unique self' -- that is, differentiated and separated from the rest of the world -- he misses the opportunity to create an identity that integrates and corresponds to the world around it. Eventually, worried Bellow, "he comes to realize at last that what he considered his intellectual 'privilege' has proved to be another form of bondage." (Harper, 1966)

The pursuit of 'just be yourself' -- the idea that you can (and should) try to make your pulses notably and distinctly different than those around you -- seems ultimately destined to take you to some very solitary places. The freedom to be an individual is, equally, freedom to exist in isolation.

And so it is that we find ourselves today: as individuals, we are architectural wonders, perplexing cellular structures composed of cells that, individually, coordinate their actions on a massive scale in order to give rise to life. Our lives, you and I as persons, must in turn figure out relationships to one another. What we collectively achieve depends on how well we syncopate our energies. Like cells in sinoatrial node, we might be individual parts, distinct units from the whole, but we only create life when we get in rhythm with one another.

REPRESENTATION

Imagine that there was a way to measure what every person in your country thought about health care. Around dinner tables, water coolers, and in waiting rooms, millions of people daily exchange their opinions about the efficiency, cost, and future of health care. But most of these statements and opinions expressed are not directly influential for many people. (Atran, 2004, p. 90)

However, if the president or prime minister makes a comment about health care, his words are beamed across the country via media reports and television screens. Every statement is then dissected by an army of pundits, theorists, and experts. Lawmakers, health practitioners, insurance brokers -- everyone has their own interpretation and agenda. Importantly, all this commentary is digested and rehashed by the people sitting around dinner tables, water coolers, and waiting rooms talking about it. Everyone interprets new input by hypothesizing its relevance to them as individuals. The averaged sum of all these ideas -- or, "public opinion" as it is called -- loops back to inform the perspectives and strategies of the highest level decision-makers. In turn, the country-wide discourse is reciprocal.

Suppose that we are anthropologists from another planet. We are here to study the behaviour of human societies on Earth.

We might describe health care as a "cultural representation". Since health care does not exist apart from its human architects, we would conclude that the institutions of human health care are ultimately representations of what people believe about themselves -- in short, their culture. In other words, health care is not only an arrangement of assumptions and institutions, it is also a symbol that represents an identity. Whether individuals believe health care ought to be expanded or shrunk, publicly funded or privatized, all "believe" something about health care. And all who engage in the discussion believe that health care is, at the very least, worth debating in the first place.

On this level, the symbol of health care is vital to all of us, because it allows us to identify ourselves as belonging to a culture, even if we might disagree on the directives or particularities of the symbol itself.

Only a fraction of what we think about health care is ever spoken or expressed. Government officials do not, generally speaking, mindlessly blurt out whatever ideas bounce across the top of their minds. Neither do you, while standing around the water cooler, generally express every thought without inhibition. Cultural representations -- whether health care, government, or religion -- are not symbolic manifestations of every minute inclination we have. In fact, most of the time we ourselves are oblivious even to our own underlying assumptions themselves. Why is this? Every thought we express about health care is processed, calculated, and mediated in our minds by the representation of health care that already engulfs us. Where did our intuitions about the nature and purpose of health care come from in the first place?

But we do much more than imitate the representations around us. As we create funding policies, hospitals, health services, and insurance coverage plans, we are not simply replicating cultural representations as we inherited them -- rather, we are adapting them. And these adaptations, in turn, evolve the cultural representations themselves.

No matter what you do today, your efforts, likewise, transpire on this morphing plane of ideas.

FLORENCE

The childhood circumstances of Pietro Perugino (1450-1523), the Italian painter, are difficult to determine with certainty. Contemporary historians argue that he came from a family of status and privilege, but his earliest biographer, Giorgio Vasari -- who has a flair for dramatic embellishments -- recounts the story of Perugino as a gruelling tale of rags-to-riches. (Stillman 2005[1896]:209)

According to Vasari, Perugino was born into dire poverty, and was forced by his father to be a drudge servant of "a not very distinguished painter" in Perugia, his hometown. However, we are told that this nameless, unknown artist inspired Perugino to study art, and kindled in him "the desire to be a great master." (Vasari, 1946[1550]:164)

Eager to learn and prove himself, Perugino often asked, "Where are the best painters?" To this inquiry, his employer would reply, "Florence [is] the place above all others where men attain perfection in all the arts, but especially in painting." (Ibid)

He gave three reasons: first, there were so many good critics there, for the air of the city makes men quick and perceptive and impatient of mediocrity; next, to succeed in Florence a man must work hard, be rapid and ready, and able to earn money, since living in Florence is expensive; and the third reason is the most important of all, that the rivalry between men of talent is there most keen. (Ibid 164-5)

Florence, Vasari tells us, was the epicentre of the art world: it forged the best artists because the competition was fierce. Rivals were "thankless for favors, harshly critical of their competitors." (Ibid) Vasari thinks of this ruthless antagonism as a refining fire, burning away the chaff of artistic mediocrity. The artist who could survive Florence would be fashioned by her.

By his descriptions of early artistic rivalries, Vasari was among the first Italian writers to use the concepts of concorrenza (competition) and concorrente (competitor) in economic terms. The fiscal realities were all too evident: to survive as an artisan required competing for business. Vasari noted that this act of competing seemed to push artistic and entrepreneurial innovation further, which, in turn, increased demand for art. (Goldthwaite 2009:390-1)

Since Florence was the hardest place in the world to be an artist, Florence was the best place in the world to become an artist.

Competition. Whether you laud it or loathe it, whether you see it as the road to our salvation or the seed of our demise, one thing seems fairly evident: competition creates environments that force us to sink or swim. An ancient Hebrew maxim says that one man sharpens another, just as iron sharpens iron. (Proverbs 27:17) Whether you are an artist in Florence, an actor in New York, a retailer in Beverly Hills, or a start-up application developer in Silicon Valley, setting up your camp alongside the competition requires you to be your sharpest.

Florence is probably exactly where you want to be. That is, set your sights on the hotbed of rivalry for your domain of labour. This is the hardest place to eke out a living, but here, in the words of Vasari, you have the greatest opportunity to "attain perfection." To become the best that you can be, choose to compete with the most excellent, admirable, and formidable contestants.

TRAFFIC SIGNAL

Imagine watching a busy city intersection for the first time in your life.

The traffic is constant, loud, and repetitive, but you quickly notice a pattern to its flow. You perceive that the traffic signal is very good at predicting the behaviour of the drivers. There is a very high probability that the automobiles will stop when they approach the intersection against a red light. Even though you have never seen an intersection before, it does not take you long to learn the pattern and anticipate the movement of the traffic:

red lights are signs -- fairly trustworthy signs -- that incoming cars will stop when presented with the signal.

Later, you find yourself in a car, behind the wheel, and driving towards the very same intersection. Now you are a direct, internal participant with the traffic's behaviour. You are no longer an external observer to what is happening. From this vantage point, you acutely realize that the traffic lights do not predict traffic behaviour (like the clouds might predict rain), but rather the red, yellow, and green signals direct behaviour. You understand the mutual obligation of all drivers to respond in conformity to the orders of the signal. It is evident that the predictability -- and thus safety -- of the whole situation depends on everyone surrendering their autonomy in obedience to the traffic light. You participate, in kind, by stopping when signalled to do so. And by this action you reinforce the collective assumption that all drivers stop at red lights. (c.f. Hart 1961:88-89)

In this scenario, obeying the traffic signal is not merely obeying a rule, it is also following established group behaviour. True, violating the traffic laws will likely get you a ticket, but the threat of this punishment is only a viable deterrent if a vast majority of drivers in your particular region actually do, in fact, stop at red lights. If the collective assumption was that traffic lights are merely decorative, there could be no reprimand enforced for not heeding them. The fact that you might get a ticket for your disobedience is a consequence of the fact that just about everyone else has agreed that red lights shall be heeded as directives.

So what is the difference between a rule and a collective behaviour? Or, what is the difference between law and cooperation? A rule that is ignored by mass noncompliance is powerless to exert any order. Could we even consider it to be a 'rule' at all? The only thing that makes something a law is that people follow it. An unfollowed law is, simply, no law at all. The law, in true praxis, is what people -- all citizens -- enable and permit one another to do collectively.

Order is, more rightly, synchrony of the majority's behaviour. Therefore, we might think of rules as being more reflective and descriptive of social behaviour than predictive of it, just as the traffic at an intersection demonstrates the unwritten, collective agreement about what shall be done at red lights.

Leaders, executives, law-makers, and managers know this all too well: individual behaviour is not so much determined by the rules and policies, but rather by how the rest of the group behaves. You can draft all the arbitrary codes and bylaws you want, but the rules we truly follow are ultimately the patterns we see in one another.

Moral Collisions

If being a capitalist means that every person has an equal opportunity to work hard and benefit from the fruits of their labour, then to this extent I am a capitalist.

If being a communist means leveraging our collective efforts and resources so that we can accomplish more together than alone, then to this extent I am a communist.

If being a libertarian means acknowledging that other people are not mine to control or coerce, then to this extent I am a libertarian.

If being a socialist means that society ought to expect from each person what they are able to contribute and provide for each person as they have need, then to this extent I am a socialist.

If being a conservative means believing that values are important, tradition has something to teach us, and freedom deserves protection, then to this extent I am a conservative.

If being a liberal means believing in generosity, compassion, and equality, then to this extent I am a liberal.

If being right-wing means that I believe in order, then to that extent I am right-wing.

If being left-wing means that I believe in movement, then to that extent I am left-wing.

The central task of any government is to mediate beliefs, balancing diverse convictions simultaneously, as if in an equilibrium of permanent tension. When a critical mass of decision-makers becomes magnetized around the pole of any one extreme (it does not matter which one), the cost is a detrimental suppression of other important values. Convictions that ought to mediate between extremes are then quelled, or even stigmatized as immoral. Ironically, a stable government is an inherently chaotic one: its steadiness comes as a result of its internally-conflicted ecosystem of competing values.

Take any ideology too far and you will eventually end up in morally dangerous territory.

In the opening sentences, I sought to demonstrate how an individual's personal array of civil ideals might be 'divided' across a spectrum of governance ideologies (and no less by the lines of partisan politics within those systems). However, the structure of most democratic governments comes with the unfortunate consequence of marginalizing the valid points of any opposing view. In the battle for votes, agreement with the other side is perceived as weakness. The tendency, or temptation, is always to focus first on the faults of your adversaries.

Democracy imposes a frustrating paradox: the ideal politician is the non-politician.

The person we want leading is the individual devoted to the endless collision of opposing moral energies, someone who will make decisions while cautiously teetering on the edge of uncertainty. But the person we elect into office is the individual who convinces us that the 'other side' is just a bit closer to moral bankruptcy than they are. It does not take too much research to discover that this toxicity has existed as long as democracy itself. It seems to be inherent to the system.

We want a leader who is determined to perpetually wrestle with the needs of the whole population along with the situations of individuals within the population. But the person we elect tends to be the individual who can most eloquently expound a silver bullet campaign slogan, a partisan policy framework that is declared will solve such-and-such a problem.

In sum, I think democracy presents a compelling lesson for all leaders: be the most cautious of your most confident decisions -- for these are the decisions of which you least grasp the counter argument.

VORACITY EFFECT

Imagine a coastal region that has been dependent on the fishing industry for decades. The oceans are considered common, international property, so the individual fishermen and businesses do not consider it their personal responsibility to worry about fish stock renewal or habitat regeneration. After all, if they do not harvest what they can, then someone from a neighbouring country surely will! Everyone believes that in order for the fishing industry to remain competitive, there ought to be no regulations or policies that prevent overfishing.

Far away, in another part of the world, another shoreline community has ratified treaties with its neighbouring countries. These bilateral agreements determine how many fish may be caught by each nation, and the boundaries in which fishing can occur. To oversee the ordinance, the countries coordinate a central enforcement agency that monitors fishing activity, and employs marine scientists to audit the life cycles of fish species and the overall health of the oceanic ecology. The highly regulated industry requires the fishermen pay taxes which, in turn, finance the whole bureaucratic machine that licenses and controls the fishing industry.

Which nation has a more efficient fishing industry?

Imagine a country governed by two or three factious militia groups. Citing deeply harboured racial and political ideologies, they regularly clash with one another along their disputed borders. In one of the regions, the remnants of a centralized government, now virtually powerless, pleas for assistance from other countries, begging for aid in order to assist thousands of displaced people suffering across the country. The international community responds, and planeloads of food and supplies are successfully flown into the capital. But the distribution channels are fragile and tedious: the aid must cross from one faction's side to the other, and the rogue 'power brokers' of the day do not hold the idea of 'sharing' as a high priority.

Somewhere else, imagine a country that is organized into multiple levels of bureaucratic governments. Citizens are taxed on the income they earn, the property they own, and the purchases they make. This tax revenue funds an extremely complex, multi-layered chain-of-command system. The governments of the provinces/states and the governments of the cities/regions are not autonomous: their responsibilities are legislated by national/federal government, which determines the rules and parameters by which tax revenue (i.e. the national budget) will be distributed across the whole country. All this depends on a rigorous process of checks and balances, which in turn creates further levels of accountability and reporting (that the taxpayer must ultimately pay for). As a result, to maintain this massive political infrastructure, hundreds of thousands of public servants are employed, salaried, and (likely) unionized.

Which nation has a more efficient manner of governance?

We often forget that even though centralized, organized bureaucracies are often inefficient, obtuse, and 'clunky', they also tend to be far more efficient than most alternatives in the long run. In the absence of structured oversight, overall resource waste surges to its highest levels. Economists Aaron Tornell and Philip Lane describe this as the 'Voracity Effect' -- it occurs when a windfall of resources is inefficiently squandered because there is no centralized authority system to effectively leverage and distribute in such a way as to benefit the economy as a whole. (Tornell & Lane 1999)

Consider what happens to the fish stock and the international aid in our above examples:

Year over year, the unregulated fishing industry will be less productive than its highly regulated counterpart. Long term, all those taxes, policies, and international treaties mean that the administrative top-heavy bureaucracy makes for a more viable and competitive fishing industry than the free-for-all, winner-takes-all approach. Simply: keeping a renewable resource renewable is an economic no-brainer.

Likewise, the guerilla-run country -- the ultimate example of an unregulated, completely 'open market' in every possible sense -- is equally inept at handling an influx of new resources. In such scenarios, international aid can be easily wasted or, even worse, be leveraged by one group to increase its domination over another. The Voracity Effect explains why some countries with massive oil reserves are also in dire economic situations: insufficient channels of authority result in newfound wealth simply being swallowed up by the power brokers, and the long-term result is worse for everyone than if the oil had never been exploited in the first place. This provides an explanation as to why a surge in a commodity export price can increase levels of poverty in a producing country, if the commodity production itself is not regulated by a central authority.

Recall the second country we discussed above -- the one with multiple levels of government and red tape. Imagine that a series of devastating natural disasters wreak havoc across this country. At the community and municipal levels, neighbours do their best to aid one another, but clearly more assistance is required. Intermediate state, provincial, or territorial governments lobby federal or national levels of government for emergency assistance, who may in turn deploy specific agencies or even military personnel to the affected areas. In dire situations, the highest head of state may even appeal to other countries for further assistance. The existence of a central chain of authority means that assistance has a far better chance of being effectively distributed than if all the levels of government were autonomous (or, at worst, competitive).

In sum, bureaucracy has its benefits. At the onset of the disaster, hundreds of protocols and policies are triggered in governmental offices across the country, across all levels of government. Resilience, whether in human communities or natural ecosystems, is created essentially the same thing: multiple layers of interdependent complexity and redundancy. The next time you are tempted to complain about the inefficiency of one organizational process or another, just ask yourself what the situation would be like in the absence of any organization at all.

I reckon that, for the most part, even the most frustrating systems are far better than anarchic bedlam.

Of course, there will always be room to improve the effectiveness and efficiency of our institutions. And there is great economic and social benefit in achieving this aim. But the point here is that we ought to remember that a bureaucracy is successful to the extent that it thwarts and diminishes the Voracity Effect. No system is perfect, but many systems are drastically under appreciated.

JEVONS PARADOX

The year is 1865. England is in the midst of the Industrial Revolution, literally and figuratively steaming ahead by its exploitation of coal power.

As the steam engine increasingly expanded trade routes and revolutionized manufacturing, personal standards of living were heightened in turn. It was clear that the 'secret' to England's booming prosperity depended on coal. William Stanley Jevons (1835-1882), a British economist, wrote:

> Coal in truth stands not beside but entirely above all other commodities. It is the material energy of the country — the universal aid — the factor in everything we do. With coal almost any feat is possible or easy; without it we are thrown back into the laborious poverty of early times. (Jevons, 1865, I.3)

Since coal was evidentially central to the nation's way of life, many people, like Jevons, were concerned with a logical and critical question: when will it run out? There was rampant speculation that England's coal reserves (and those of her primary trading partners) were rapidly nearing depletion.

> This question concerning the duration of our present cheap supplies of coal cannot but excite deep interest and anxiety wherever or whenever it is mentioned: for a little reflection will show that coal is almost the sole necessary basis of our material power, and it is that, consequently, which gives efficiency to our moral and intellectual capabilities. (I.6)

To avert the depletion of coal, some of Jevons' contemporaries suggested that increasing the efficiency of coal-powered machinery could, at the very least, slow the rate at which it was mined. "It is very commonly urged," wrote Jevons, "that the failing supply of coal will be met by new modes of using it efficiently and economically." (VII.1) However, Jevons believed that this strategy was fundamentally flawed: if the nation became more fuel efficient then the price of coal would go down, which would then lead to an overall increase in consumption, since coal would then be cheaper.

> It is wholly a confusion of ideas to suppose that the economical use of fuel is equivalent to a diminished consumption. The very contrary is the truth. (VII.3)

Hence, Jevons' paradox: increasing efficiency leads to increased consumption. Considering the economy as a whole, he pointed out that better coal efficiency would not diminish the amount of coal used, but rather the efficiency would generate more economic growth that would, paradoxically, simply end up burning more coal in the long run.

Another popular argument in Jevons' day was that newer steam engines would be so fuel efficient that they would only require a fraction of the coal demanded by older generations of engines. High expectations were placed on future innovations to massively reduce coal consumption, thereby supposedly reducing the nation's degree of coal dependency. Not so, retorted Jevons: more fuel efficiency will only foster more consumption:

...an improvement of the engine, when affected, will only accelerate anew the consumption of coal. Every branch of manufacture will receive a fresh impulse— hand labour will be still further replaced by mechanical labour, and greatly extended works will be undertaken... (VII.21)

...no one must suppose that coal thus saved is spared —it is only saved from one use to be employed in others, and the profits gained soon lead to extended employment in many new forms. The several branches of industry are closely interdependent, and the progress of any one leads to the progress of nearly all. (VII.26)

In modern day economics, the overall impact of Jevons' paradox is a bit more complex: to understand the full degree of the paradox's impact on the consumption of resources and commodities, one must also account for taxation, levies, conservation policies, and other values and cultural factors that can help keep the price of a resource arbitrarily high, thus forcing a decrease in its actual rate of consumption.

At a personal level, consider how Jevons' paradox affects our most precious commodity: time. Think about the effort we exert to 'save time' through efficiencies, systems, gadgets, and productivity. We are constantly on the hunt for a better steam engine: the next app, device, or management theory that will require just a little bit less fuss, tweaking, and input than the current one. When we find it, we herald the new efficiency; this, we declare, will finally save us some time!

Paradoxically, the things that save us the most time end up demanding the most. Here, where economics meets chronemics, we must confront the uncomfortable realization that the more adept we are at using something efficiently, the more of it we use in the long run.

If you want to burn through more time, just become more productive.

FRACTALS

The trunk of a tree divides into branches, which divide into sub-branches, which divide into twigs.

Water trickles from a puddle into a stream, which merges into a river, which merges into the ocean.

Blood from the heart travels through the aorta, which divides into arteries, which divide into capillaries.

The same branching 'fan out' pattern exists in the bronchioles of your lungs and dendrites of your nervous system.

If you 'zoom in' on a tree, you discover that a single, tiny twig shares the same basic structure and form of the whole tree, just smaller. You could think of the twig as a "fractal" of the tree, a term coined in 1975 by Benoit Mandelbrot (1924-2010) to describe the geometry of nature. The natural world, he proposed, is not random at all, but it follows "strict order" self-similar, geometric properties. (Mandelbrot, 1977:17) Thus, fractals provide a mathematical framework to measure the ratios and scales of ecological life.

Nature, honed for efficiency, works predominately in these kinds of scaling, self-replicating patterns. Life is created by repeating the form of itself at numerous scales of detail.

In the domain of human invention and systems, our designs tend to follow similar fractal patterns:

Traffic from an expressway merges on to avenues, which divide into streets, which divide into driveways.

Decisions are made in boardrooms, disseminated through departments, assigned to teams, executed by individuals.

The data of an email message travels between routers, to a server, to a local network, to an email client.

Biological life is created as cells replicate themselves. The social and cultural lives we create for ourselves are, likewise, inherently self-replicating. A country is like a bigger version of a city, which is like a bigger version of a neighbourhood, which is like a bigger version of a family. A family, in turn, is like a bigger version of an individual -- who is composed of mutually dependent cells giving rise to life. And yet, at the microscopic level, a single eukaryote cell looks like a bustling, complex metropolis, full of labour divisions and communication protocols.

Here, in the world of fractals, we discover that everything is like a copy of something else.

ORGANIZING OURSELVES

ALEXANDRIA

The Library of Alexandria was a famous library, nestled somewhere along the shoreline of the ancient Egyptian port city. Although its exact location has never been determined, the legends of this royal institution have continued to echo through the Western tradition of ideas and stories.

According to the fragments handed down to us, the library was established early in the reign of the Ptolemy dynasty, sometime in the third century BCE. Even less is known about its destruction. Multiple sources blatantly contradict one another, leaving even the century of its demise uncertain. The present-day historian is left with little more than the faculties of conjecture to hypothesize what actually happened. One way or another, the general consensus is that the library was destroyed by fire. Who lit the first spark, when, and why, are all mysteries furiously debated in circles of historiography.

Before its destruction, the library was said to be the ancient world's centre of thought and education. It contained "400,000 mixed rolls and 90,000 single, unmixed rolls," as described by John Tzetzes (1110-1185), one of our primary sources, and the earliest author to provide a description of the collection. (Lapidge 2006:8) Tzetzes himself, however, lived centuries after the library's destruction. Even our best sources depend on traces of legend.

Roger Bagnall (b. 1947) is a classical scholar who is skeptical about the scale and size of the library as told through its evolving legends. For him, the postulation of such a grandiose institution says more about our ambitions today than it says about an actual institution in the ancient world. In spite of a glaring lack of concrete evidence, the image of the Library of Alexandria continues to persist in our imaginations -- an idea that we retroactively paint upon the past. This is why Bagnall thinks of Alexandria as a dream we cannot escape: "No one, least of all modern scholars, has been able to accept our lack of knowledge about a phenomenon that embodies so many human aspirations." (Bagnall 2002: 348)

We might think of the library itself is an iconic, universal symbol of the whole human enterprise. We are archivists at soul. The human psyche longs for foundational reference points; anchors to which we can declare our allegiance and cite in confidence. All libraries provide this manner of foundation: whether publicly funded institutions, personal collections on a bookshelf, canons of spiritual reflections, selectively curated folders on a digital device, or even lists of Internet bookmarks. Libraries give something that we can point to and say, "Here: this is my framework of understanding and this is the justification of my beliefs, at least thus far." Likewise, in the context of communities, libraries represent our common stock of knowledge; our shared points of understanding.

We know very little about the great Library of Alexandria, but we do know why it was, and is, important to us.

SOCIAL INTELLIGENCE

In 1966, after spending over four hundred hours observing lemurs in Madagascar, primatologist Alison Jolly (b. 1937) developed a thought-provoking theory about the origin of animal intelligence.

Earlier, in 1962, R. J. Andrew, an assistant professor at Yale University, had suggested that a species' intelligence evolved by adapting to the ever-shifting game of predator and prey: as one species evolved strategies for avoiding its predators, the predators were likewise forced to evolve to survive -- a continual, reciprocal process. (Andrew 1962:587) For Andrew, this cycle of predator-prey adaptation provided the evolutionary basis of intelligence in mammals and primates. The original recipe for the evolution of cleverness is that generation after generation of species had to outsmart one another in the contest of survival.

But after hundreds of hours observing lemurs, Jolly found herself thinking about animal intelligence in a different light. She noted that a lemur is required to learn a lot from his troop; a young lemur must not only learn his clan's warning signals when predators are spotted, but he also must learn the rank, order, and idiosyncrasies of others in his community. Lemurs live in complex societies, which require young lemurs to be socialized and "educated" with information that is specific to their troop. This prompted Jolly to make a broader observation: a primate "takes his cue from others of his own species, as much or more than from the predator's behavior." (Jolly 1966:505)

Jolly turned prior assumptions about intelligence on their head. Instead of accepting that primates evolved intelligence first and then formed complex social communities second, she argued that social life itself was the basis of intelligence. Mental capacity did not evolve as the result of the predator-prey cycle, but the real driving force behind the evolutionary formation of the intellect is that species that can understand, communicate, and structure themselves in hierarchical orders tend to survive. For Jolly, socialization is the engine behind intelligence: "primate social life provided the evolutionary context of primate intelligence." (Ibid 506)

Consider the incredible social intricacies of our own human intellects: we can hypothesize the outcomes of multiple potential actions and choose between them; we can not only sense the agency of others, but we can even speculate what they are thinking; we can conjecture the likely reactions of others to our actions, even before we do them; we can infer, theorize, and surmise. According to Jolly, these social capabilities are not the result of evolving a higher intelligence, but rather social demands themselves resulted in the intellects we have today.

If Jolly's thesis is correct, the intellect is an inherently social phenomenon -- social intelligence is our first intelligence. We became so adapt at sensing the behaviour of others that we learned to turn our sensing and hypothesizing capabilities to the rest of the world. Science, art, and the imagination itself -- everything finds its intellectual origin in our ability to relate to one another as a species.

CLEVERNESS

Why do other animals not learn mathematics? Why don't other primates perform Shakespeare or play SimCity? In short, why are humans as clever as we are? This was the question put forth in an influential 1976 essay by psychologist Nicholas Humphrey (b. 1943), who pointed out that from a purely evolutionary perspective, it appears that we humans are far more clever than we need to be to survive.

Humphrey defined intelligence as 'modifying behaviour on the basis of valid inference from evidence.' (Humphrey 1976) Thus, a species exhibits intelligence when it develops new methods, strategies, and techniques for accomplishing tasks, like hunting, foraging, navigating, etc. With the exception of the hominids, such behaviour modification occurs extremely slowly in the animal kingdom, usually over the span of many generations at a time. Humans, in relative terms, modify their behaviour quickly. Why? What incited this capability?

At some point in our distant past, our ancestors were like every other species in the sense that we lived in clans, acquired food, avoided predators, and procreated. And then something happened. Somewhere in our ancient lineage, we set out on an adaptive track that would eventually enable us to colonize every continent, exploit resources deep underground so that we could fly jetliners across the oceans, and singlehandedly protect or eradicate other species, virtually at our will and whim. The million dollar question: why did nature let us happen?

One day Humphrey was watching some monkeys in lab cages. He watched a mother and child negotiating the perils of weaning, younger monkeys play fighting, and adults grooming and socializing. And in a moment he realized that the origin of advanced intellectual capabilities was unfolding right before him: perhaps we acquired our ability to manipulate and respond to the world because we lived in social contexts that forced us to respond to and anticipate one another. The story of human evolution is not only about adapting to the environment, it is just as much about adapting to each other.

Hence, Humphrey's proposition: the better we became at anticipating, predicting, and sensing the ambitions, actions, and motivations of others, the more complex our brains became... and as social environments became correspondingly more complex, intellectual demands increased as well. Thus, stated Humphrey, "I propose that the chief role of creative intellect is to hold society together." (Ibid)

Furthermore, Humphrey surmised that our inherited social intellect is what predisposes us to interacting with nature herself as if she is a conscious, feeling entity: when we "bargain" with the laws of physics through ritual and prayer, we are essentially applying our socially-wired cleverness to manipulate the wills and emotions of agentless forces. We misappropriate our intellectual ability by trying to negotiate relational transactions outside of relational domains. Our inclination for the supernatural is simply our desire to treat nature as if she was ontologically like one of us.

On the other hand, the scientific method is equally an application of human initiation on nature, but instead of exerting our will upon her, the experimenter begins from a position of listening, sensing, and examination. Our empirical capabilities are equally rooted in social adaptation of the intellect, but they approach nature with the assumption that she is not a relational or rational creature to be bartered with.

In sum, magic and science both begin with the same relationally-inspired impulse of human intellect, but they diverge in practice, just as our capacity to understand and manipulate one another are like different sides of the same coin.

Noble Savage

Echoing through the centuries there are two common (yet compellingly contrary) ways of thinking about human nature. In the first view, we find ourselves in the Garden of Eden together: here, freed from the arbitrary forces of the state and institutions of control, we harmoniously celebrate a state of common respect and concern for one another. Such an image is conjured by John Dryden's 1672 play, The Conquest of Granada, wherein a character named Almanz announces:

Obeyed as sovereign by thy subjects be,
But know, that I alone am king of me.
I am as free as nature first made man,
Ere the base laws of servitude began,
When wild in woods the noble savage ran.
(Dryden, 1672, p. 40)

This is the underlying assumption of the 'noble savage' motif: beneath the facade of state-based society, humans are naturally predisposed towards living together in peace and mutual cooperation. Philosophically, proponents of the noble savage have argued that humanity's path to order and decency is returning us to our innate, 'pre-civilized state' of compassion and concern. Like the noble savage, they implore us to rise above the rules of competition, which they indict as the handmaidens of sovereign states and greedy rulers.

Juxtaposed to the legacy of the noble savage, we find Thomas Hobbes' (1588-1679) interpretation of human nature. For Hobbes, humanity has little innate nobility: without rulers "to keep them all in awe," human populations will disintegrate into war -- cyclical clashes of war of "every man against every man." (Hobbes, 1651, XIII.8) Therefore, humanity, in its most 'natural state', is hopelessly bleak:

there is no place for industry, because the fruit thereof is uncertain, and consequently no culture of the earth, no navigation nor use of the commodities that may be imported by sea, no commodious building, no instruments of moving and removing such things as require much force, no knowledge of the face of the earth; no account of time, no arts, no letters, no society, and, which is worst of all, continual fear and danger of violent death, and the life of man solitary, poor, nasty, brutish, and short. (XIII.9)

In Hobbes' view, industry and organization -- the antidotes to humanity's natural bent for violence and aggression -- necessitate rulers and ruling structures. Central to Hobbes' concern was how such institutions could be established and elected, for he was convinced that they were imperative requirements for achieving any semblance of peace and security.

So what is human nature, really? If we were all left to our own moral devices, would we 'default' into peace-loving savages or warmongering retaliators?

Lending supporting to Hobbes' perspective, some theorists argue that the average likelihood of men dying because of human-to-human violence can be up to sixty percent higher in present day 'tribal' societies than in 'modernized' societies. (Keeley, 1996) Archeologists point to ancient mass graves that appear to be the result of extremely violent conflict among early hominids. (Thorpe, 2003) Of course, surrounding all these propositions is no small degree of debate as to what counts as admissible evidence and justifiable inference.

Similarly, some draw a comparison between the violent behaviour of chimpanzees, our close genetic relatives, noting their capacity for violence as an analogue with the human propensity for conflict. (Smith, 2009) However, in advocating for humanity's naturally peaceful nature, the social and promiscuous bonobo is often presented as evolutionary justification for our own primordially collaborative and cooperative nature. (Ryan & Jethá, 2010; also see Prüfer, et al, 2012)

It seems that asking whether the essence of humanity is fundamentally good or evil is like asking whether human behaviour is the consequence of nature or nurture -- unable to clearly tease them apart, the most appropriate answer seems to be a tentative yes to both. Maybe, as the old metaphor goes, there are two wolves, Good and Evil, battling it out inside of each of us.

Perhaps, in all this, the question ought not be: 'what have humans become?' but rather, 'what can humans become?' Maybe the fact that we can argue about our genetic relationship with chimpanzees and bonobos indicates that we have the capacity to imagine our behaviour beyond the mere restraints of ancestry and inheritance? The most compelling element of the human story is not what we have been, nor what we are, but rather, what might lay ahead for us.

I know of no philosopher who has yet been so bold as to say: this is the limit of what man can attain and beyond which he cannot go. We do not know what our nature permits us to be. (Rousseau, 1763, p. 62)

Human nature: a work that is still in process? Who we are today is not a laurel to rest upon, but a foundation from which to reach higher.

ORIGINAL SIN

The theological idea of 'original sin' owes much to Augustine (354-430). Broadly speaking, the notion of sin is clearly a common theme in the Bible, and early Christian theologians had already invested much speculation on the nature of sin, but Augustine is recognized as the first to effectively systematize sin as a doctrinal point of order.

For Augustine, the logic went something like this: every human being needs redemption; hence, infants also require divine forgiveness through baptism. Therefore, since infants require redemption, then they too must be carriers of a sinful nature, for they have not yet wilfully done anything sinful.

Therefore, all humans, including infants, are marred by sin and thus evil by nature. (Wiley, 2002, p. 60)

> Hearken, O God! Alas for the sins of men! Man says this, and You have compassion on him; for You created him, but did not create the sin that is in him. Who brings to my remembrance the sin of my infancy? For before You none is free from sin, not even the infant which has lived but a day upon the earth. (Augustine, Confessions, Book I, Chapter 7, 11)

Augustine's reasoning may be counterintuitive to us today, but his idea has had no small degree of influence on our world. He rested his case on Romans 5:12, which states that "just as sin entered the world through one man, and death through sin, and in this way death came to all men, because all sinned." Thus, even though the actual term "original sin" is never itself used in the Bible, theological exegesis culminated in a doctrine which explicitly declared humanity's "moral deformity" and blamed Adam and Eve for this "hereditary stain." (Harent, 1911)

So influential was Augustine's argument that on June 17, 1546, the following decree was issued and "original sin" became an impenetrable ecclesiastical doctrine. Now, denying the existence of original sin warrants excommunication from the church itself:

> If anyone asserts that the transgression of Adam injured him alone and not his posterity, and that the holiness and justice which he received from God, which he lost, he lost for himself alone and not for us also; or that he, being defiled by the sin of disobedience, has transfused only death and the pains of the body into the whole human race, but not sin also, which is the death of the soul, let him be anathema. (Council of Trent, 1546)

Following Augustine, Protestants would overwhelmingly affirm this stance. In fact, it could be argued that the doctrine was taken even a step further by the Reformer Martin Luther (1483-1546) to include the utter and "total depravity of man." Luther wrote,

And if they be not justified, they are sinners. And if they be sinners, they are evil trees and can do nothing but sin and bring forth evil fruit—Wherefore, "Free-will" is nothing but the servant of sin, of death, and of Satan, doing nothing, and being able to do or attempt nothing, but evil! (Luther, 1525, p. 55)

...If, therefore, Christ be the Lamb of God that taketh away the sins of the world, it follows, that the whole world is under sin, damnation, and the devil. (Ibid p. 125)

John Calvin (1509-1564) wrote,

We thus see that the impurity of parents is transmitted to their children, so that all, without exception, are originally depraved. The commencement of this depravity will not be found until we ascend to the first parent of all as the fountain head. We must, therefore, hold it for certain, that, in regard to human nature, Adam was not merely a progenitor, but, as it were, a root, and that, accordingly, by his corruption, the whole human race was deservedly vitiated. (John Calvin, Institutes of the Christian Religion, II.1.6)

...Original sin, then, may be defined as a hereditary corruption and depravity of our nature, extending to all the parts of the soul, which first makes us obnoxious to the wrath of God... (Ibid II.1.8)

Today the Catechism of the Catholic Church still affirms:

By his sin Adam, as the first man, lost the original holiness and justice he had received from God, not only for himself but for all human beings. Adam and Eve transmitted to their descendants human nature wounded by their own first sin and hence deprived of original holiness and justice; this deprivation is called "original sin". (Catechism of the Catholic Church, 7.416-417)

Every human, born evil. For the non-believer, the concept seems psychologically corrosive, if not detrimental. Imagining that every newborn baby literally inherits the sin of Adam (as incurred for his rebellious eating of a piece of fruit) is a proposition far beyond the realm of comprehensibility for many people today. Furthermore, convincing young children that they have inherited this 'sinful nature' might be considered by some as downright emotionally abusive.

At the same time, however, we might also ask: what does the history of original sin tell us about ourselves as a species? Whether or not you think of our systems of government, justice, and ethics as strategies to thwart our theologically 'sinful nature', these institutions are nonetheless founded on the understanding that it is better for all of us if we force one another to not give in to every compulsion and desire. Perhaps the truly most remarkable trait of our 'human nature' is not our greedy rebelliousness and sinfulness, but rather our insistence on having creeds and definitions to order our collective behaviour. Ironically, maybe the story of 'original sin' is actually a story about a 'human nature' that demands a moral code. Perhaps we are not so depraved after all.

Lex Naturalis

> ...there is a general idea of just and unjust in accordance with nature, as all men in a manner divine, even if there is neither communication nor agreement between them. (Aristotle, Rhetoric 1.13.2)

Over the centuries many great thinkers have speculated and theorized about the existence of natural law. Such a moral code, it is said, is plainly evident, just as the physical laws of nature are clear to anyone who investigates them. "What nature has granted to man," wrote Cicero (106-43 BCE), is a mind to comprehend the "connection between men" and "natural fellowship among them." From here, "the source of laws and right can be found." (Cicero, De Legibus, 1.16-17)

Later, theologians would see a parallel between the existence of perfect, natural laws and the perfect, supernatural God who created them. Augustine (354-430), one of the most influential early Christian thinkers, wrote that there is an "eternal law which is pressed upon our nature: It is the law in virtue of which it is just that all things exist in perfect order." (Augustine, De libero arbitrio I.6.15) Picking up on this theme, Thomas Aquinas (1225-1274) wrote:

> the light of natural reason, whereby we discern what is good and what is evil, which is the function of the natural law, is nothing else than an imprint on us of the Divine light. It is therefore evident that the natural law is nothing else than the rational creature's participation of the eternal law. (Summa Theologica, II, Question 91, Article 2.)

This notion of natural law has profoundly shaped our world. "We hold these truths to be self-evident," begins the American Declaration of Independence -- hinging on the assumption of natural law as its founding principle. The primary author of the document, Thomas Jefferson (1743-1826) also wrote extensively about the existence of natural law, the basis of the "self-evident" truths around which a society ought to be established:

> I appeal to the true fountains of evidence, the head and heart of every rational and honest man. It is there nature has written her moral laws, and where every man may read them for himself. (Jefferson 1854[1793]:613)

A notable critique of natural law theory later came from a British philosopher named John Austin (1790-1859). Austin considered laws themselves to be morally neutral. He did not assume that laws exist because morals are divinely etched or encoded into humanity. Rather, he proposed that the 'natural' aspect of law is that human societies simply have a 'natural' propensity for adhering to sovereigns and rulers:

> The existence of law is one thing; its merit or demerit is another. Whether it be or be not is one enquiry;

whether it be or be not conformable to an assumed standard, is a different enquiry. A law, which actually exists, is a law, though we happen to dislike it, or though it vary from the text, by which we regulate our approbation and disapprobation. (Austin 1995[1832]:157)

Following Austin, the floodgates of criticism were opened on the theory of natural law. What if two societies have conflicting or contradicting laws and yet both claim that their laws come from God? How can the truth of a natural law be verified if it is only determined rationally? What happens when natural laws are interpreted differently?

Austin argued that laws are first and foremost a social construction: human laws exist only because humans make them, enforce them, and obey them. Morality and legality thus become separate debates. Just because something is a law does not automatically make it ethical, no matter how the existence of the law is justified.

Does the natural world innately show us the right way to live? Or do we make laws in order to organize ourselves in the natural world? Every time you encounter a rule, law, or policy, your interpretation, obedience, or disobedience rests on the way you perceive the nature of law itself. This perennial debate exposes some deeply ingrained assumptions about authority that will directly affect the way we live today.

LAW

The British jurist John Austin (1790-1859) described law as synonymous with command: orders to do (or not do) specific things. He reasoned that every command must have a commander, and every legitimate command must include an adequate degree of threat to guarantee compliance; a command means that "you are able and willing to harm me in case I comply not with your wish." (Austin 1885:89) Therefore, he concluded that every society (even modern democracies) must obey a sovereign -- someone, past or present, who originally issued the command that everyone conforms to through their adherence to the law.

In Austin's theory, the reason you do not break the law today is because you are living in submission to the sovereign of the state. The sovereign may be the orders of your patriarchs, the decrees of your constitutional founders, or even currently elected representatives of your legislature.

Austin's most notable critic was H.L.A. Hart (1907-1992), a law professor at Oxford University. Hart argued that Austin's theory of law was too simplistic: it was like equating law to a gunman who holds you up and demands that you surrender your wallet. (Hart 1961:6) Hart believed our relationship to law was much more nuanced and complex than the sheer threat of punishment. We do not simply obey the law because we are obligated to do so, but rather because law-abidance is an intrinsic aspect of human behaviour. Apart from the formal laws of the land, human culture is filled with duties, expectations, taboos, and common morals that do not have any political enforcement. (Ibid p. 56) Rules are inseparable from human organization. Thus law-abidance is more than the fear of punishment; "the normative structure of society" seems to reflect a much more complicated array of factors. (Ibid p. 86)

All the same, Austin's original thesis provokes an intriguing question: what, exactly, is law? From the criminal code to the tax code, none of these rules simply originated out of thin air. We might consider a constitution or a legislative assembly as the source of our laws, but why do we, today, insist that the original architects of these documents, archived procedural bylaws, or bloodline relatives still ought to govern us?

We do not primarily abide by legal rules; we abide by customs and traditions that declare who will govern us.

Austin thought that if you keep pulling back the layers, eventually the idea of law itself appears to resemble something like a cultural habit or ritual. And, if you follow the regression dependencies back far enough, it seems that every constitution or official legislation ultimately depends on an unwritten idea or belief to establish its authority. For any country or state to be ruled by law, somehow a majority of the citizens must come to the belief that the laws are real. It is not simply a question of 'Who makes the law?' The question is, 'Who determines who makes the law?' And this is a question of belief, not legal code. Even if you yourself became the author of the laws -- the supreme ruler of your state -- your authority would still no less depend on the right people 'believing' in your rulership.

The question to ask ourselves today is not, 'What is the law?' nor even, 'Who made the law?' but rather, 'Why do we believe in the existence of laws in the first place?' For without our collective belief in them, do laws even exist at all?

TZEDAKAH

Tzedakah comes from the Hebrew word for justice. Quite different from contemporary notions of charity, tzedakah was generally taught to be practiced as a religious obligation, a code or a law to be adhered to.

One of the most famous teachings about tzedakah comes from the medieval philosopher Maimonides (1135-1204). In *Hilkhot Matanot Aniyim* (laws about giving to poor people) he describes eight 'degrees' of tzedakah, the highest decree of which "is to strengthen the hand of a Jew who is poor, giving that person a gift or loan or becoming a partner or finding a job for that person, to strengthen the person's hand, so that the person will not need to ask for assistance from others."

If you are not in a position to assist people by helping them acquire employment or a self-sustaining income, you are instructed to follow the second degree of tzedakah: give to the poor. However, you as the giver must be "unaware of the recipient, who, in turn, is unaware of the giver." (Mishneh Torah, Hilkhot Matanot Aniyim, 10:7-14) In this way, tzedekah is anonymous: "the righteous give in secret and the poor profit in secret."

Recall a similar teaching by Jesus:

...when you give to the poor, do not let your left hand know what your right hand is doing, so that your giving will be in secret... (Matthew 6:3-4)

Secret generosity is also a central theme in legends of Saint Nicholas, a fourth century Greek bishop who was said to place monetary gifts in the shoes of his parishioners when they were not looking. Nicholas, of course, is understood to be the original source material for the Santa Claus mythology.

On one hand, the Judeo-Christian tradition of 'covert giving' seems to have waned over time: we wear branded t-shirts for charity fundraiser campaigns, name our institutional buildings after their benefactors, and print larger-than-life cheques for photo-ops and media releases. However, this may be confusing terms and definitions: it is probable that Maimonides and Jesus meant something quite different in their descriptions of giving than our present day notion of charity.

Tzedakah, justice, is ultimately the reflection of a state or community's capacity to care for its members with blind equity. In a sense, tzedakah is more akin to dutifully paying your taxes than donating to a nonprofit. Unlike participating in a run for some charitable cause, remitting taxes is both compulsory and confidential. The government does not send you a t-shirt exclaiming, "Look at me, I support taxation!" because, at its most rudimentary level, it is the duty and expectation that everyone will contribute their part to the 'common purse' of society. Tzedakah implies a similar notion: justice is not something for which you receive an invitation to 'opt in'; it is simply expected of everyone.

Granted, it is not common to think of 'justice' and 'taxes' as synonyms. Taxes are generally considered in a quite negative light: ominously, "the taxman cometh," we equate "death and taxes" with one another, and many people, at best, are skeptical, perhaps justifiably worried that their tax dollars are simply funding the next scandal as the Sheriff of Nottingham makes a concerted effort to rip them off.

Regardless of where you find yourself on the political spectrum, nowhere is it currently popular to describe taxation as a positive thing. The present, prevalent narrative is that taxation is a cause of social problems, not a part of their remedy.

However, taxation is analogous to tzedekah in the sense that it legislates all citizens to contribute to a commonly shared infrastructure. Hospitals, roads, schools, utilities, law enforcement, fire protection, libraries, cultural centres, public spaces, national security -- from the township to the national level, such institutions drastically level the playing field for every citizen. Institutional commons are the bedrock of equal opportunity, the door into which every person can theoretically get a foot. Through its expenditure of tax revenue, every nation demonstrates its particular interpretation of justice: for some nations, health care is a basic human right; for others, the use of roadways is allowed only for those wealthy enough to pay the tolls. Whose responsibility is it to pony up the cost of secondary or post-secondary education, the individuals who access it or everyone in the community?

In this sense, every budget is a moral document; an ethical declaration stating how pooled monies shall be leveraged. What are we morally obligated to provide for one another? Every nation interprets this ethical responsibility in varied, unique, and complex ways. (Internal political wrestling between privatization and publicly held goods reflect the specific issues of present contention in every community.)

The fundamental question is this: what do we collectively believe is deserved by everyone, regardless of their particular social status in our community?

Taxes are like tzedakah, and tzedakah is like justice: a personal obligation to certain moral rights which are to be held equally by all. Our taxes -- this compulsory donation to the commons -- is our society's practical declaration of what 'equality' actually means to us in practice.

LAWEIPLEIN

You have probably never heard of Hans Monderman (1945 -2008), but he was a trailblazing revolutionary in the world of traffic engineering and urban design.

In the centre of Drachten (a Dutch city in the province of Friesland) there is a four-way intersection known as the Laweiplein. Prior to 2001, the Laweiplein was similar to just about every other major intersection: traffic lights, concrete mediums, directional arrows, and signs -- lots and lots of signs. The intersection also had a reputation for being dangerous, which prompted Monderman to rethink the conventional wisdom of road design.

In an effort to make the Laweiplein safer, Monderman proposed a counterintuitive solution: remove all the signs. He also put a circular grass knoll in the centre of the intersection, thus creating an uncontrolled roundabout. The result was an intersection that caused drivers, cyclists, and pedestrians alike to feel a little less safe -- thus forcing everyone to slow down, heed one another, and pay attention. The rates of collisions and injuries decreased notably.

Monderman theorized that lights, signs, and signals invite drivers to effectively stop thinking, since they turn the act of driving into an act of passively following rules. He argued that the status quo of road design is counterproductive: operating a motor vehicle ought to demand focussed attention, not invite passive obedience. Ordering traffic through commands and signals leads to a predictable situation, "When you treat people like idiots, they'll behave like idiots," he said. (Vanderbilt 2008:26)

There is an element of libertarian thinking in Monderman's philosophy. He was, in fact, a strong believer that society's responsibility to form moral values was unnecessarily hampered by the political interference of legal constraints. However, his ethos for road design was rooted in a more encompassing vision: "I don't want traffic behavior, I want social behavior." (Ibid 31)

When automobiles are travelling at 32 km/h, about 5 per cent of pedestrian collisions result in a fatality. If the automobile is travelling over 48 km/h, the fatality jumps to 45 per cent. And if the vehicle is traveling at 64 km/h, the fatality rate is a whopping 85 per cent. Interestingly, corollary studies indicate that we know this initiatively: cyclists and pedestrians report feeling the safest around vehicular traffic moving at about 30 km/h. (Hamilton-Baillie 2005:44)

In a sense, about 32 km/h is our maximum "human speed". A young adult running downhill, full-tilt, pretty much maxes out at around 30 km/h. For millions of years, it was impossible for us to go any faster. We might imagine this as our human speed limit -- the fastest we can go by our own propulsion. Interestingly, it is virtually impossible for us to maintain eye-contact with another person if we are separated by a speed differential of more than 32 km/h. (Ibid)

When an intersection forces motorists, cyclists, and pedestrians alike to slow down to 32 km/h, the place begins to exhibit more social behaviour than typical "traffic behaviour". By removing all the barriers between pedestrians and motorists, Monderman's confusing and ambiguous intersection forced all travellers to slow down to a "human speed" and, as a result, the space became a safer place for everyone involved. Rule-following gives way to dynamic interactivity, like social interactions, as the space demands awareness and cognizance of other individuals.

Clarity -- signs, rules, signals, and barriers -- increase speed. And the more you trust the cues, the less you need to pay attention. Perhaps in a similar way, personal decisions are often the victims of haste: the more informed you feel, the less contemplation you exercise. But, like an intersection, the more dangerous a decision feels, the more attention you pay to the details. Eliminate all the comfortable barricades and markers; force yourself to keep your head on a swivel.

PEACE

Martin Luther (1483-1546) and Huldrych Zwingli (1484-1531) were two Reformation theologians who disagreed vehemently with each other. Point of contention: the interpretation of Christ's statement "This is my body" uttered at Holy Eucharist.

Zwingli argued that "This is my body" ought be understood in a metaphorical sense, and should not be connotative of the actual presence of Christ in the bread. He wrote, after carefully reviewing scripture, that "we are compelled to confess that the words: 'This is my body,' should not be understood naturally, but figuratively..." (Zwingli, 1530)

Luther, even though he had rejected the Catholic doctrine of transubstantiation, did not go as far as Zwingli. For Luther, the Eucharist was still no less a co-union (communion) with the divine, an act of eating categorically different than eating any other physical substance. Luther was so adamant that he even accused Zwingli of acting on behalf of the devil:

> Our adversary says that mere bread and wine are present, not the body and blood of the Lord. If they believe and teach wrongly here, then they blaspheme God and are giving the lie to the Holy Spirit, betray Christ, and seduce the world. One side must be of the devil, and God's enemy. There is no middle ground. Now let every faithful Christian see whether this is a minor matter, as they say, or whether God's Word is to be trifled with. (Luther, 1526)

Luther and Zwingli met face to face to confer in 1529, but reconciliation between the two proved impossible. Their disregard for the other did not diminish in the least. (As a historical footnote, their inability to resolve this dispute was indicative of the split between Lutherans and Protestants, which exists to this day.)

Another theologian of the time, John Calvin (1509-1564), was righteously enraged by the lack of respect between Luther and Zwingli. For Calvin, such antagonism between Christian believers was unrepresentative of the love of Christ. He wrote:

> Both parties failed together to have patience to listen to each other, in order to follow truth without passion, wherever it might be found. I deliberately venture to assert that, if their minds had not been partly exasperated by the extreme vehemence of the controversies, the disagreement was not so great that conciliation could easily have been achieved (Armstrong 2007:173)

Calvin sounds like an angel of mediation in this context, but he himself had his own doctrinal squabbles. Despite his disillusionment with Luther and Zwingli's hatred for each other, Calvin was vehemently opposed to a man named Michael Servetus (ca.1509-1553). Servetus argued that belief in the Trinity -- that is, the creed God the Father, Son, and Holy Spirit are of the same essence -- was unbiblical. Rather, he proposed, there is only one God alone and that Jesus, while still divine, was not equal to God the Father. This enraged Calvin, who still believed that the Catholic creed of the Trinity ought to be carried by the Reformers.

February 13, 1546. In a letter to another friend, Calvin famously wrote, "Servetus has just sent me a long volume of his ravings. If I consent he will come here, but I will not give my word for if he comes here, if my authority is worth anything, I will never permit him to depart alive." (Rives 2008:291)

August 13, 1553. Servetus is arrested in Geneva.

August 20, 1553. During Servetus' trial, Calvin wrote, "... after he had been recognized, I thought he should be detained... I hope that sentence of death will at least be passed on him; but I desired that the severity of the punishment be mitigated." Calvin argued that Servetus ought to be beheaded, not burned at the stake. "We sought to soften the kind of death but we were frustrated," he wrote. (Ibid 292-3)

October 27, 1553. Servetus was burned at the stake as a heretic, charged with blasphemy against the Trinity and denying the legitimacy of infant baptism.

June 21, 1555. Standing before his congregation, John Calvin preached: "Therefore, you must be gentle with others. Now, this is not only for God's service but also out of common charity which ought to be applied between neighbours, whether or not they are subordinate to us." (Calvin, 1555)

Supporting the execution of a theological opponent while simultaneously preaching love, forgiveness, and compassion appears to be the epitome of hypocrisy. How is it that Calvin could press for the death penalty while advocating Christ's call to be gentle with one another?

The history of religion is riddled with recurring versions of this dilemma.

The unavoidable conundrum of religion is that it is a continual argument about how to achieve peace.

And, throughout human history, we see the same pattern over and over again: our arguments about how to achieve peace are usually the most violent debates we have.

Calvin's vision of neighbours living together in compassionate concern was founded on a substrate of theological axioms. Central to his understanding of love, was a set of foundational beliefs about the nature of Jesus. The two were inseparable. Thus, in Calvin's mind, the heretic who attacked the foundational doctrines attacks peace itself. And here we meet the disconnect: in the name of love and truth, perpetrators must be eliminated -- even by violence, if necessary.

Here in the twenty-first century, it is all too easy to glance over our shoulders and mock such misguided, medieval morals. But perhaps our self-righteousness is not entirely justified. We might think of Calvin's acceptance of violence as a means to theological unity as analogous to accepting violence as a means to political unity. Ultimately, colonialism, terrorism, and imperialism all have, at the end of the day, the very same aim:

instituting a particular order that will guarantee peace, security, and justice.

The conflict is not between 'good' and 'evil', as if they were squared off against each other as opposing moral forces; it is between competing visions and versions of peace, justice, and security.

If I do not accept your conviction and recipe for peace -- whether it be American constitutionalism or Sharia law, for instance -- then I will, eventually, seek to exert my dominance over your way of life, an agenda which inevitably will give me legitimate grounds to exercise force.

How can you fight for peace without kissing violence?

Today, as in the sixteenth century, it is all too easy to overlook this perennial human dilemma. Tie together all your most cherished beliefs: like freedom, compassion, fairness, gentleness, and so on. Now ask, Is there anyone -- anyone at all -- to whom these values do not absolutely apply right now?

Like John Calvin, in defence of the greater good, most of us are quite happy to eliminate the antagonists to our particular version of peace.

TELOS

At the beginning of the *Nicomachean Ethics*, Aristotle observes that all human activity is driven by some intrinsic goal or aim. (1.1.1) In Greek, the word is *telos* (τέλος). The telos of the objects around you is easy to figure out: the telos of a die is to be rolled; the telos of a chair is to support the person sitting on it. The function of every object corresponds to its design. What, then, is the telos of a human being?

To answer this question, Aristotle suggests that we begin by determining what makes us different from every other creature. He concludes that our unique trait is defined by our ability for rational contemplation. The telos of a lion chasing its prey is to catch dinner, but the lion is not choosing or reflecting upon its actions. Aristotle believes that humans, on the other hand, are innately rational, reflective creatures, capable of thinking about their actions and beliefs beyond instinctual response.

Furthermore, Aristotle asks, what do we suppose that the gods themselves actually do all day? Surely their primary occupation -- their "divine activity" -- is thinking itself...

> the activity of God, which is transcendent in blessedness, is the activity of contemplation; and therefore among human activities that which is most akin to the divine activity of contemplation will be the greatest source of happiness. (10.8.7)

> A further confirmation is that the lower animals cannot partake of happiness, because they are completely devoid of the contemplative activity. The whole of the life of the gods is blessed, and that of man is so in so far as it contains some likeness to the divine activity; but none of the other animals possess happiness, because they are entirely incapable of contemplation. Happiness therefore is co-extensive in its range with contemplation: the more a class of beings possesses the faculty of contemplation, the more it enjoys happiness, not as an accidental concomitant of contemplation but as inherent in it, since contemplation is valuable in itself. It follows that happiness is some form of contemplation. (10.8.8)

For Aristotle, the telos of humanity -- the highest activity to which you and I can aspire -- is to engage in rigorous contemplation: to engage our minds as fully and wholly in our activities and decisions as we are able. There is no higher call. This is our aim. It is for this that the gods will reward us:

And it seems likely that the man who pursues intellectual activity, and who cultivates his intellect and keeps that in the best condition, is also the man most beloved of the gods. For if, as is generally believed, the gods exercise some superintendence over human affairs, then it will be reasonable to suppose that they take pleasure in that part of man which is best and most akin to themselves, namely the intellect, and that they recompense with their favors those men who esteem and honor this most, because these care for the things dear to themselves, and act rightly and nobly. Now it is clear that all these attributes belong most of all to the wise man. He therefore is most beloved by the gods; and if so, he is naturally most happy. Here is another proof that the wise man is the happiest. (10.8.13)

Aristotle's quest for humanity's telos echoes a question that seems to have been around for as long as we have consciously moved on the earth: why are we here? His response is compelling: we're here to do what other living creatures cannot do, namely, lead lives of reflective contemplation.

We are also the only species to build acropolises and drive sports cars... are these activities, then, also a part of our purpose? I wish I could ask him this question.

Instead, we are left to only imagine his response. I think he would say, "Well, how do you choose between building an acropolis and driving a sports car on any given day? If you must choose, and there must be some reason, and if there is a reason, then there must be an end (telos) to your choice." It all comes back to depth of thought.

In his own words,

> if we do not choose everything for the sake of something else (which would obviously result in a process ad infinitum, so that all desire would be futile and vain), it is clear that this one ultimate End must be the Good, and indeed the Supreme Good.

What do you think? Is contemplation our Highest Good?

AIMS

"An agent does not act except for some end," wrote Thomas Aquinas. (Summa Theologica, I.5) All around you, people, machines, and other animals seem to be bustling about their purposes, as if animated by the pursuit of their goals. Everyone, or, should we say, everything, seems to have a telos, a directive, or at least an ambition. What is action if not a striving for a goal?

Rush hour. Grocery stores. Television. You see them everywhere: agents acting purposefully, presumably doing their task as a means to one end or another.

Even the quiet, solitary gentleman sitting on the park bench -- he is probably just trying to relax. What is a vacation except a valiant effort to recover from the strenuous toll of life's other efforts? Everyone has an agenda, all the time!

Or at least it seems that way.

On the other hand, if you stop us on the street (interrupting our little missions in progress) and ask us to describe our purpose and aims in life, our responses are often quirky and disjointed. We'll talk about something to do with our families, or maybe mention some upcoming product launch, or speculate on our options for furthering education.

You know, masked confusion.

It seems like most of us have fairly foggy visions of the future. In fact, if pressed for an honest answer, we cannot even predict our futures with any degree of certainty. Even those of us who claim to have concrete plans in place will usually admit, perhaps with some prodding, that the plans we have today are not the same plans we had five years ago. Who has faithfully and unremittingly pursued the same teloi all their life? In truth, we know that our aims and goals must remain fluid enough to adapt to reality as we go along.

Thus, it is amazing how much rampant ambiguity lies beneath the surface of our neatly coordinated hustle and bustle.

As Aquinas said, we certainly appear to be agents on a mission. But do any of us really know what the mission is?

Frankly, life often makes the most sense at the level of the milk run -- a telos driven by the straightforward ambition to assure that tomorrow's breakfast will include the proper ingredients. Explaining the purpose of a single trip to the grocery store is much easier than explaining the purpose of why I am alive and consuming said groceries in the first place.

If we were to truly give ourselves an intractable and immovable purpose for being here, I imagine that we would crumple under the pressure. The field trip to the grocery store would become an exhausting abstraction: "We must feed ourselves, providing nourishment for our cells so that we can accomplish such-and-such a great thing with our short lives!" instead of, "We're hungry, let's eat something delicious!" My guess is that having a sole and singular purpose for life would kind of ruin everything: a Great Purpose would arrest all the other wonderful intricacies and idiosyncrasies of life and make them handmaidens, the means, to its insufferable agenda.

So while an existential contemplation about the metaphysics of the grocery store is all well and good, it risks the danger that we miss the quirky beauty of life by trying too hard to explain everything. Of course, I do not mean we ought to abandon critical reasoning -- no fewer problems await us on that end of the pendulum. Rather, I propose that we not neuter the joyous ridiculousness of the present by insisting that everything around us is subservient to some little plan we have concocted and superimposed on life.

Don't miss out on today by trying too hard to explain it.

The Helpful and the Hurtful

Maxim of Benevolence

Immanuel Kant (1724-1804), one of the most preeminent figures of philosophy, described the moral responsibility individuals have to one another:

> The maxim of benevolence (the practical philanthropy) is the duty of all men towards one another; whether they be found amiable or not, according to the ethical law of perfection, Love thy neighbour as thyself. (Kant 1799:37)

However, as Kant explains, 'Love thy neighbour as thyself' is remarkably more complicated than it might seem at first. Kant is especially concerned about how acts of benevolence are perceived by a person living in poverty:

> we acknowledge ourselves to be under an obligation to the beneficent towards a poor man; but, as this kindness comprises dependence of his weal upon my generosity, which however humbles him, it is duty to spare the receiver a humiliation by a behaviour,

which represents this beneficence as either what is merely owed, or a small service of love, and to preserve for him his reverence for himself. (Ibid 35)

If our generosity towards someone in need is disrespectful or humiliating, we have in fact broken the maxim of benevolence: we do not want to be disrespected or humiliated; therefore we ought not bring shame to the recipient of our benevolence. Kant is extremely sensitive to this dilemma. He solves the problem by arguing that true benevolence is not an emotional or even altruistic act. Rather, the one who helps another ought to simply see themselves as "obliged" to assist, and "honoured" that the recipient accepted their offer:

He must also carefully avoid every appearance as if he thought by this to bind the other; because it would not else be a real benefaction, which he conferred on him, by discovering that he intended to impose an obligation on him (which always humbles him in his own eyes). He must rather appear as if he himself were either obliged, or even honoured by the other's acceptance consequently as if the duty were what he merely owed , if he does not (which is better) exercise his act of beneficence quite in secret. (Ibid 40)

For Kant, all this comes back to treating his neighbour the way he wants to be treated: "I will the benevolence of every other towards me; I ought then to be benevolent towards every other." (Ibid 37)

If both parties (the giver and receiver) know that the other would do same for them if the roles were reversed, then the power dynamic of the giver over the receiver is drastically diminished. By emphasizing this obligation to help one another, Kant removes the likelihood that the recipient will feel indebted or "bound" to the giver. Therefore, in Kant's scheme of things, benevolence is only benevolent inasmuch as it eliminates all gushy displays of charity and pretences of generosity. Instead, Kantian benevolence presents an attitude of, "Seriously, this is just my duty. It isn't even a choice." In Kant's own words: "the duty of mutual benevolence according to the principle of equality, (all others on the same footing with me) [allows me to] will well to thyself, on condition that thou willest well to every other; because in this manner only thy maxim (of beneficence) is qualified for a universal legislation, in which all law of duty is founded." (Ibid 37-38)

Perhaps the greatest exemplar of humanity is the person who selflessly assists their neighbour in need. However, simultaneously, such assistance risks inciting a power differential that might, in turn, lead to a cancerous erosion of trust. Kant was acutely aware of the power of charity to potentially undermine the social fabric of a community. Therefore, he advocated that we view benevolence as code of conduct, not as a volunteer activity. If benevolence could be 'legislated' it would not carry an air of superiority around with it anymore.

Today, his reflections invite us to probe the motivations and strategies that inspire our own benevolent deeds.

IATROGENESIS

The physician must be able to tell the antecedents, know the present, and foretell the future -- must mediate these things, and have two special objects in view with regard to disease, namely, to do good or to do no harm. (Hippocrates, Of the Epidemics 1.2.5)

"I will do no harm," states the Hippocratic Oath. This creed was reinvigorated in the seventeenth century by an English physician named Thomas Sydenham (1624-1689), who was likely the first to Latinize the motto, *primum est ut non nocere.* (Smith 2005:372) To this day, *primum non nocere* -- "first, do no harm" -- remains a pillar of medical ethics.

Since the dawn of medicine, doctors and practitioners have been acutely aware that treating a patient is risky. Every healer is a human, prone to miscalculation, hence the ever-present possibility that a course of treatment might bring about a calamity of counterproductive consequences.

In medicine, the word for unintended and inadvertent harm is *iatrogenesis*, literally meaning 'brought forth by the physician'. It epitomizes a doctor's greatest fear: instead of fostering health and recovery, the patient becomes a victim of yet another infliction -- the doctor. Whether a combination of prescribed medications interacts to create an injurious concoction, or a hospital-acquired infection is contracted, or negligence and malpractice are to blame, the recipient of an iatrogenic treatment faces a daunting realization: their present state might be better if they had simply not received medical care in the first place.

The pursuit of 'not doing harm' demands that a physician be constantly careful, critical, and ever-learning. The status quo must especially remain under an eye of weary suspicion. For hundreds of years, bloodletting was practiced with the best of clinical intentions: it conformed 'logically' to observations of menstruation and secretions (after all, it was abundantly evident that bodily fluids were expelled after their usefulness). For generations, bloodletting was universally understood, accepted, and promoted as an effective remedy. However, over the centuries, the practice severely harmed millions of patients -- proving that even the most obvious and conventional strategy to help can actually be detrimental. Bloodletting is a textbook case study of iatrogenics. Just because a practice is universally accepted does not mean it is somehow inherently free of harm.

Unlike physicians, most of us are not charged with the task of making life and death decisions every day. But, like physicians, we are still no less the architects of outcomes we produce today, entirely regardless of the intentions we profess for our actions. An abiding, chronic trait of the human condition is the lingering potential that we can inadvertently cause harm while seeking to foster life. There is never a guarantee that the fruits of our labours will match the intentions of our efforts. In life, as in medicine, this foundational ethic eternally pleads with us to second-guess even our most sacred assumptions: first, do no harm.

BEST INTENTIONS

"We came here to make things better, but maybe we have made things worse."

This thought still echoes in my mind. It came as I was walking through a small village in the Dominican Republic several years ago. I was visiting the town along with a team of child sponsors; individuals contributing monthly donations to provide schooling and basic nutrition for many of the children in the town. We had come to meet the children we were supporting and to assist in the construction of a new school. A team of doctors in our group held medical clinics.

As it turned out, sponsoring a child for thirty dollars a month can create situations that are far more complex than the humanitarian brochures had suggested. For the donor, the equation is quite simple: set up an automatic withdrawal from your account, receive a tax receipt, and feel good about doing something positive in the life of a child. All this, as the adverts proclaim, for less than the price of a coffee a day! However, this is only half the story.

Local residents explained that volunteer help at the school had decreased significantly since the sponsorship dollars started rolling in. Our 'support' was powerfully disincentivizing: if wealthy folks from far away are going to pay for running the school, why should we bother getting involved? Without any critical research or forethought, we had set the precedent: when you have problems, rich First World citizens will come and fix them for you.

We had exposed our underlying Western assumption: we solve problems by throwing money at them.

It was also evident that our donations had affected the social dynamics of the town. Some children were accepted into the school program, but others were not. The political bureaucracy behind this selection process was far beyond our privy, but it only existed because we were funding it in the first place. Imagine a stranger visiting your childhood neighbourhood and arbitrarily giving millions of dollars to some of your friends' college funds but not to others. It does not take a great deal of imagination to guess how this might affect the relational fabric of a community. We had, in effect, introduced a class system.

Just because an idea is driven by really good intentions, does that make it a good idea?

The hardest actions to bring under the spotlight of scrutiny are the actions most deeply rooted in our best intentions.

Once we believe we are acting for the highest good, a critical evaluation of our work drastically undermines our sense of moral agency in the world. In fact, honestly evaluating what we already believe to be the highest good is pretty much impossible, since we have already enthroned it as the highest good in the first place.

This story is not only about a small village in the Dominican Republic. Traces and subplots of this story show up around the world.

... There is mounting evidence suggesting that indiscriminately pouring aid into a country greatly hinders the recipient nation's manufacturing and export sectors over the long run. Arguably, perpetually providing aid actually keeps nations poor. (Rajana, 2011)

... After the January 12, 2010 earthquake in Haiti, the subsequent importation of rice from donor countries came dangerously close to destroying the local Haitian rice market itself. (EMMA Rice Report, 2010)

... Some economists argue that many African countries have not been able to establish self-sustaining textile industries because they are inundated with donated t-shirts and clothing from the West. (Frazer, 2008)

... Anthropologists, such as Erica Bornstein, argue that when children are enrolled in monthly sponsorship programs, "new perceptions of economic disparity are produced by the very humanitarian efforts that strive to overcome them." (Bornstein, 2001).

... The issue of governmental corruption is a vexing dilemma: when resources are diverted into the pockets of corrupt politicians and bureaucrats, away from those who are most desperate, the continued desperation of the poor attracts further aid funding which, in turn, is also absorbed by the corrupt heads of state. The result: "according to some measures of corruption, more corrupt governments receive more aid." (Alesina & Weder, 2002)

When it comes to humanitarian efforts, we naturally react out of a sense of moral responsibility, not detached, neutral evaluation. This is to our collective benefit to be sure: thankfully, most of us have an emotional tripwire that incites us to help our fellow human when we are exposed to the cruelty of his suffering. The problem is that the moral circuitry runs so deep that we cannot second-guess it. The pattern is ironic, but seemingly unavoidable: to the extent that we ascribe moral valour to our agendas, we subsequently fail to subject our agendas to moral inquiry. (Little surprise, then, that history is rampant with the stories of the greatest evil being done in the name of the greatest good.)

When you are giving everything you can to help another person, the single hardest question to ask yourself is, "Am I really helping?" And yet, to the degree that you genuinely care -- the degree to which your help is not merely a self-validating affirmation of your own ego -- is the degree to which you might learn about the endless other factors contributing to their plight. And sometimes, sadly, it might mean accepting that one of the contributing factors is your own misguided attempts to alleviate the problem on their behalf. But if we do in fact care about the suffering of others, we must be willing to drag our own mistakes into the sunlight. Then, and only then, can we learn, together, how to move forward effectively.

Justice and Charity

Let us consider the difference, should there be any, between equality and charity.

Equality is not a gift. You cannot give it to me. Equality only exists to the degree that we both have it already. It is non-transferable.

If you have equality and I do not have equality, then equality clearly does not exist in the first place.

If you suppose that your charitable actions towards me are 'giving' me equality, then you are assuming that equity is a possession that is in your ability to bestow on others. Moreover, if you expect me to express thankfulness to you, demanding that I acknowledge your gracious gift, then you betray your assumption that you are, strangely, somehow 'more equal' than me. (If you give me a gift, it is quite appropriate for me to express my thankfulness to you. But I cannot thank you for 'making' me your equal.)

Equality can only be recognized, never bestowed.

What, then, do we make of our highly publicized and glamourous humanitarian pursuits to 'bring dignity to the downtrodden' and to 'lift up those who are oppressed'?

Could it be that we have forgotten justice in our pursuit of charity?

Could it be that equality is a fruit of justice, not a result of charity?

> If they are different, either the just or the equitable is
> not good; if both are good, they are the same thing.
> (Aristotle, Nicomachean Ethics, 5.10.1)

A world of charity, by necessity, would be a world of inequality: for as long as there is charity there is a 'handing down' from the donor to the recipient.

Would a world of justice, by necessity, be a world of equality? Does justice make charity obsolete? Is charity merely a temporary polish to cover over the residue of injustice? Does charity perpetuate and reinforce the strata of inequality? Do we assume that we can give away enough charity to create equality?

Is justice or charity your greater concern today?

LEADERSHIP IN THE HIVE

LEADERSHIP DOODLE

This is one of my favourite napkin doodles:

I draw a circle to represent "a goal".

Another circle to represent "the people".

An arrow pointing from the "people circle" to the "goal circle".

The question: what is leadership?

What does it mean to move people — the rather finicky creatures that we are — to actually do something together?

Push. It seems that some leaders get behind the people circle and push it towards the goal. Well, they call it "encourage," actually. Nelson Mandela said, "It is wise to persuade people to do things and make them think it was their own idea." (Stengel, 2008) Classic push-leaders often find second careers as motivational speakers: "Yes, you can do it!" is their primary message.

Pull. Some leaders get in front of the people circle and pull everyone along, in a way that conjures up the stereotypical image of an alpha personality, akin to the image of a face-painted

William Wallace persona leading the charge. In less euphoric times these are the leaders who, in the words of John Naisbitt, settle for "finding a parade and getting ahead of it." (Naisbitt, 1982) When they are actually sitting still they are busy fine-tuning endless drafts of vision, purpose, objective, and mission statements.

Insiders. Some leaders like to dive into the people circle and lead from within. Disciples of Dale Carnegie and John Maxwell come quickly to mind. These are the people who are out to save corporate America one coffee appointment and "checking in on you" email at a time. Of course, we all love these kinds of leaders – and we know full well that these leaders love for us to love them too.

If I am the crunched up end of a coffee stir stick, bouncing around the metaphorical napkin of leadership, I find myself most in sync with my convictions when I just ignore the people circle altogether and move myself toward "the goal" circle. Trying to manipulate and alter people's thinking (not to mention their habits) is hard work, in fact it is a never-ending pipe-dream into which one can easily flush many years.

Ironically, most of the leaders who we revere as our idols did not invest their lives into trying to subvert the conscious landscape of the people circle. No, the greatest leaders in history seem to have just gone after the goal because they believed in it. The following hypothesis lands outside of the realm of provability, but perhaps it carries anecdotal truth nonetheless: humans seem almost lustful to follow an individual with an audacious, personal commitment to practical action.

We instinctively want to trust leaders who are really going to "make it happen" -- so it seems logical that there is no leader more enticing than the one who is already doing it. We know that the leader who cares the most is the leader who will die for the goal, even if no one else is following. Yet, these are the people who become the magnetic centres of movement, change, and accomplishment.

The adage is as old as the hills: if no one follows you, you are not really a leader. The problem is that most people who call themselves leaders do not really know if anyone is following them. They are too busy trying to create alignment -- something about getting the right people on the right seats on the right bus. You can invest so much energy into managing, motivating, and manipulating the people circle in the name of "leadership" that the actual task itself is forgotten in the pile of self-help books.

"Leadership" has become more of a psycho-persuasion exercise than doing an action that other people repeat, mimic and respond to in turn.

Doers. As an alternative to general push, pull, and insider models of leadership, I want to suggest a third idea: go and do it and see who follows you. To really test your leadership capacity, quit trying to lead people and actually try doing "the thing" you want others to do. If people come along then you have followers -- then and only then are you truly a leader.

The first concern of the leader is the goal circle, not the people circle. Yes, you should care deeply and genuinely for your followers — caring for those around you is indispensable — but don't confuse your "followers" with people who you are merely trying to coerce into doing something that they would never find you yourself doing.

Leadership, as a methodology, sells a lot of books.

Leadership, as a job title, is an institutional invention.

Leadership, as a discipline, is the pathway to dogmatism.

Leadership, as an ideal, is the instigator of disillusionment.

Leadership, as a status symbol, breeds resentment.

Leadership, in a reality, will simply change your neighbourhood.

CHANGE THE WORLD

Making a difference -- from securing wealth for our offspring to accumulating converts to brand --provides us with a dearly precious mechanism for measuring our worth. Many of us seem to assume that our temporal life is only really meaningful to the extent that there is value added to the world by our existence on it.

After all, if absolutely nothing changed as a result of us being here, was there ever a point to the visit?

And so, we repeat our mantra to one another: "Just one person -- yes, you! -- can make a difference!"

Your ideas, your values, your vision; a part of the unique, idiosyncratic traits that comprise your existence, somehow indelibly etched on to the world. A difference, left in the wake of your life, like the ripple of a speed boat skimming over a lake: reverberations expanding far beyond the scope of your mortal life, exponentially fanning out through the nodes of humanity like a contagion.

You can make a difference.

For the whole world?

Yes, in fact, we say, "You can change the world."

At the same time, we cling to a contradictory, variant belief; an inertial kind of hope: we are desperate to believe that change is hard and slow. Like the new construction project that bulldozes our childhood playground, or the morphing pillars and norms of society's moral conviction, our reaction to changes wrought upon us is usually marked with distrust, suspicion, and nostalgic despair.

The desire for stability and order fosters another guiding motivation for most of us. We long for a world immune to change; a peaceful world that stifles the mad, vindictive lunatic -- where his capacity to "make a difference" is muted, truncated. Consider our institutions of government: arguably, a primary purpose of a democracy is to assure that any one person does not hold power in perpetuity. The practical function of political bureaucracy is to enforce laws that effectively suppress the degree to which one person -- namely, a 'terrorist', 'criminal', or an 'anarchist' -- can "change the world" to reflect their own agenda. Maintaining order and nurturing peace requires curtailing every individual's capacity to simply change the world as they so see fit.

Absolute peace and absolute freedom are chronically incompatible bedfellows.

After all, do you really want to live in a world where any person could actually mould the world in the image of their own desire? Imagine: what if every person alive believed that they really could "change the world" -- and what if it was true? The whole world, then, simply comprised of millions of willy-nilly agendas clashing into each other, unbounded and combustible. Unrestrained change leads to either dispersion or combustion -- neither of which reflect much of our ideal notions of society. On this level, it is not really true that "one person can make a difference" -- otherwise the most deranged individuals would have ordained chaos ages ago.

It is greatly to the benefit of each individual in society that society itself makes it exceedingly hard for any one person to "really make a difference".

However, most of us, it seems, do in fact want to see change happen in the world, but we are generally far more reluctant to open ourselves up to the change that others want to incite in us. We want to be the authors of change, not the pages upon which change is written. Because of this, the human world is not unlike a fortress built against the ever present threat of transformation. The inertia of the status quo towers over the individual, immobilizing his ambitions for crafting the utopia of his dreams.

Therefore, enacting change and being a difference-maker is profoundly harder than our desktop clichés and motivational screensaver quips would have us believe. Many orders of magnitude harder. Our insistence on reciting quotes and slogans does not guarantee that we can, in fact, actually change anything.

Let us consider two individuals: a humanitarian who wants to "change the world" by lifting people out of poverty, and a terrorist who wants to "make a difference" by enacting revenge or inciting fear in the name of a political or theological ideal. Both face a difficult mission: ours is not a world where the aims of any single individual can too easily shift the momentum of history.

The agendas of the humanitarian and terrorist stand as moral opposites, but both individuals share a common, compelling drive to incite change in the world. And changing the world, they soon discover, ultimately requires changing the minds of other humans. The only way to change anything beyond their immediate physical proximity (which is pretty much limited to rearranging the furniture) is to somehow alter broader social patterns of beliefs, assumptions, and prejudices. Ultimately, for both, change becomes a matter of reshuffling the synapses in as many other people's minds as possible.

Whether rearranging the strata of economic distribution, transforming the population's convictions about the divine, financing the redevelopment of a geographic location, or convincing the multitudes to purchase a widget, changing the world means changing minds -- lots of minds.

World-changers are mind-changers.

And that's the kicker: on average, just about everyone else is as resistant to changing their mind as you are to changing yours. Multiply this aversion to change by the population you seek to transform, and the task of "changing the world" bears its ruthlessly demoralizing, unscalable ratio of improbability. And yet, I imagine that it was from such a place of utter, honest discouragement that the philosopher William James penned this revitalizing hope:

> I am against bigness and greatness in all their forms,
> and with the invisible molecular moral forces that
> work from individual to individual, stealing in

through the crannies of the world like so many soft rootlets, or like the capillary oozing of water, and yet rending the hardest monuments of man's pride, if you give them time. The bigger the unit you deal with, the hollower, the more brutal, the more mendacious is the life displayed. So I am against all big organizations as such, national ones first and foremost; against all big successes and big results; and in favor of the eternal forces of truth which always work in the individual and immediately unsuccessful way, under-dogs always, till history comes, after they are long dead, and puts them on top. — You need take no notice of these ebullitions of spleen, which are probably quite unintelligible to anyone but myself. (James, 1899)

Today, all we really have is the capacity and opportunity to influence one another. This is all we have ever had. The matter of "making a difference" and "changing the world" are simply questions of scale, for little changes the social sphere, save for our conversations, discourses, friendships, interactions, and collective strategies for thriving in our respective environments. But the ends are not predetermined, nor is success such a thing as to be scripted in advance. Thus, perhaps the question is not whether or not you will be an agent of influence, but rather: what will you impart to your fellow agents of immeasurable, imperceptible, yet steady, global change?

DUET

In 2008, researchers from McGill University designed an experiment to determine how musicians synchronize with one another when playing a duet. (Goebl & Palmer, 2009) Sixteen highly trained pianists were divided into pairs, and each pair was given three original musical compositions designed specifically for the experiment. To collect precise data, a digital keyboard was used to record each session, along with motion sensors attached to the musicians heads and fingers to measure their response times, span of movement, and rate of non-auditory cueing.

One pianist was instructed to play a leader (soloist) part, while the other was instructed to play a follower (accompanist) part. Each pianist wore headphones, allowing the experimenters to test different scenarios: how does the pattern of synchronization change when both the lead and accompaniment can hear one another, versus when the leader cannot hear what the accompanist is doing? How does non-verbal communication between the musicians compensate for decreased levels of auditory feedback? How does the number and ratio of notes between two musicians affect their capacity to synchronize?

The experiment provided a millisecond-by-millisecond dataset of each musical performance, which could then be analyzed and compared in order to determine the musicians level of synchronization. Not surprisingly, the most precise levels occurred when both pianists could hear what the other was playing.

When the lead musician cannot hear the accompaniment, the leader's timing is quite precise. However, the follower's timing is much less accurate. Simply put: the follower makes more errors when the leader can not hear them. Incorrectly overcompensating for rhythm variability means that the follower adapts their timing much more than the leader.

But what happens when each musician can hear the other one? The data suggests that the assigned roles of leader and follower altogether disintegrate when both musicians can hear one another. Synchrony evenly distributes the responsibility of correcting timing variabilities between both musicians. When in synchrony, it is virtually impossible for one performer to 'lead' and another one to 'follow' because every note occurs in reciprocally balanced and interdependently determined rhythm.

A duet or ensemble might prompt a subtle, reflective question for those of us in leadership. Synchrony between people does not happen without a dynamic feedback system. And yet, the clearer and more effectual the feedback loop becomes, the more the lines between leader and follower seem to blur. Leaders, we might ask ourselves: to what degree do we value synchrony compared to rank?

Leadership is indeed a mysterious art and a befuddling paradox: If a leader or soloist is thoroughly out of sync with their followers or accompanists, how could the title of 'leader' accurately describe their role? On the other hand, if a leader or soloist is thoroughly in synchrony with their followers or accompanists, does the category of 'leader' even remain a valid descriptor? Leadership is unenviable partly because it is inherently asynchronous. Perhaps this is why leadership is so often associated with power: it, too, never exists where ownership and equity are evenly distributed.

What are your leadership aspirations? Are you seeking to deliver a spotlight solo performance or a synchronous duet?

FESTINA LENTE

The Roman historian Gaius Suetonius Tranquillus (69 - ca. after 122) famously undertook the task of chronicling the first twelve successive emperors. His set of biographies, *The Lives of the Caesars*, is not only a primary source for understanding the ancient Roman world, but also a channel through which several nuggets of wisdom have been transfused through Western history.

Regarding Caesura Augustus, Suetonius writes

He [Augustus] thought nothing less becoming in a well-trained leader than haste and rashness, and, accordingly, favourite sayings of his were: "More haste, less speed"; "Better a safe commander than a bold"; and "That is done quickly enough which is done well enough." (Suetonius, De Vita Caesarum, Life of Augustus, 25.4)

To describe anything done in haste, he said, "It was sooner done than asparagus is cooked." (87.1)

The Greek saying, "more haste, less speed," or alternatively, "make haste slowly," is a paradoxical saying found in several other ancient sources as well.

Suetonius describes "more haste, less speed" as prioritizing the quality of a work above the timeframe taken to accomplish it. In other words, the speed at which something should be accomplished ought to be dictated by the time it takes to accomplish it well. There is no time-oriented deadline, only a quality-oriented deadline. Thus the saying does not mean "Hurry up and wait," but rather, "Hurry up and take your take your time to be precise."

Whether we work on mechanized assembly lines, on tables with handwoven textiles, or in trenches of computer code, the same dilemma seems to hold true across all human endeavours: increases in speed tend to cause decreases in quality, and vice versa. To balance the two, we use a third-party metric called 'efficiency' to design systems that give us the best optimization of both -- an acceptable degree of quality delivered on an acceptable timetable.

But if the saying is true that "You can't rush perfection," then it is foolish to stand behind Rembrandt and tell him to hurry up on that painting... he will be finished when he is finished, and no sooner.

In other words, efficiency and excellence are not only two different words, but they mean two different things. Today, be careful lest one of them demands an unworthy sacrifice of the other. Make haste slowly.

CUNCTATOR

The year is 217 BCE. Rome and Carthage have just begun what is to be a long, gruelling, seventeen year war. The Carthaginian military, led by Hannibal, inflects massive causalities on the Roman army at Lake Trasimene, and in the process kills consul Gaius Flaminius in battle.

Back in Rome, the Senate acutely realizes the gravity of the situation: Hannibal's approach appears unstoppable. In a time of unprecedented crisis, the Senate elects an older, experienced consul named Fabius Maximus to the role of dictator.

Fabius realizes that meeting Hannibal in open battle would simply be suicidal. Refusing direct confrontation, he employs an attrition strategy by using small military detachments to wreak havoc on Hannibal's supply lines. This long-game, skirmish-oriented approach -- and refusal to engage in decisive battles -- quickly grew unpopular in unsettled Rome. Before long the people went about "denouncing Fabius, not as a weakling merely, nor yet as a coward, but actually as a traitor." (Plutarch, Lives, Fabius 8.3) But according to his biographical record:

> Fabius endured the situation calmly and easily, so far
> as it affected himself, thereby confirming the axiom
> of philosophy that a sincerely good man can neither
> be insulted nor dishonoured. (10.2)

Fabius' term as dictator ended a year later. The Romans, impatiently demanding the final defeat of Hannibal, elected two new Consuls (Paullus and Varro) who advocated the abandonment of Fabian's wait-and-delay strategy. Subsequently, in the summer of 216 BCE, the Roman army marched on Carthaginian's troops in the Battle of Cannae. Hannibal, significantly outnumbered, executed a tactical maneuvere that is still studied to this day, and crushed the Roman advance. The defeat was so acute that several allied cities defected to Carthage in surrender.

Back in Rome, the news of calamity heightened the panic. Fabius, who had once been seen as a coward, now appeared to possess the wisdom of a deity. Until his death in 203 BCE, Fabius continued to persist on his tactics of proto-guerrilla warfare to wear down the overpowering Carthaginian army. He believed that avoiding the temptation to achieve decisive victories in open battles was the only way to secure a final victory in the long run.

Fabius Maximus has a unique historical legacy: he is known for what he did *not* do. The Roman poet, Quintus Ennius, declared "one man, by delaying, restored the state for us" -- *unus homo nobis cunctando restituit rem.* (Ennius, Annales 363) Thus Fabius is known to history as the Cunctator, that is, The Great Delayer. "....his caution was prudence, and that his never being quick nor even easy to move made him always steadfast and sure." (Lives 1:4) Even today, there is a whole canon of military principles known simply as the "Fabian strategy".

Beyond military strategy, Fabius' ideas bring a renewed perspective on today's world of productivity gurus and apostles of efficiency. The Cunctator reminds us that there is often wisdom in delaying: sometimes it is more efficient to not demand efficiency. In other words, procrastination has a place. In fact, sometimes it might be the best option. Fabius realized that the invading Carthaginian army, while tactically superior in many respects, had weaknesses that could only be exploited through a waiting game. Patience is an imperative part of every strategy, even though it can easily be drowned out by the roars of people demanding instantaneous results.

SIRENS

To the Sirens first shalt thou come, who beguile all men whosoever comes to them. Whoso in ignorance draws near to them and hears the Sirens' voice, he nevermore returns... (Homer, Odyssey 12.36-44)

...they were fashioned in part like birds and in part like maidens to behold. And ever on the watch from their place of prospect with its fair haven, often from many had they taken away their sweet return, consuming them with wasting desire; and suddenly to the heroes, too, they sent forth from their lips a lily-like voice. (Apollonius Rhodius, Argonautica 4.891–919)

According to Homer, the hero-king Odysseus desired to hear the legendary songs of the Sirens, but he had been warned by a muse as to their deathly affects. As Odysseus prepared to sail past earshot of the Siren's lair, he instructed his men to tie him to the mast of his ship, and he filled the ears of all his crew with wax.

> So they spoke, sending forth their beautiful voice, and my heart was fain to listen, and I bade my comrades loose me, nodding to them with my brows; but they fell to their oars and rowed on.

Odysseus, overcome by the Sirens' songs, struggled to break free and desperately tried to convince his temporarily deaf crew mates to loosen his bonds. His men, remaining true to their original orders, simply added more ropes to bind their seduced leader even more securely.

> But when they had rowed past the Sirens, and we could no more hear their voice or their song, then straightway my trusty comrades took away the wax with which I had anointed their ears and loosed me from my bonds.

Far from the shores of ancient mythology, "Ulysses pacts" occur in present day medicine as well: when a person suffering from a mental illness is "deemed to be competent and in remission," he is able to grant permission for future treatments to be administered if he is incompetent, uncooperative, and blatantly refuses care down the road. (Puran, 2005:42)

As you look at the navigational charts for your voyage today, determine the islands of temptation that lay along your route. Ulysses pacts are decisions made when you are free to choose, that self-limit your ability to make future decisions. They are self-imposed restrictions that anticipate the possibility that your will may be thwarted by the beautiful songs of deadly distractions.

Sometimes the only way to impose your will is to surrender your ability to choose.

TITANIC

What might have happened had the Titanic not met her tragic end? It is easy to suppose that the Titanic may have been a 'success' and become the model for bigger, future ship designs. The subsequent generation of ocean liners would have doubtlessly derived and copied many of her engineering and design characteristics, seeking to increase the grandiose capacity of the vessel even farther. Instead, the Titanic exposed numerous flaws in the passenger seafaring industry and necessitated the implication of new protocols. As a result, the overall safety of transoceanic travel grew substantially because of the Titanic. Her fateful demise, as tragic as it was, contributed to the implementation of measures that surely saved many future lives. (Petroski, 2004)

Disasters such as the sinking of the Titanic expose our weaknesses, and, as evidenced over and over again in architecture, engineering, and aviation, these discoveries often come at a monumental price.

But the greater the disaster, the greater its morals and legacies influence the future. Disasters demonstrate, albeit painfully, areas that require improvement. They force us to calculate new variables, they shine a spotlight on our blind spots, and they hold us accountable for our past shortcuts. Disasters are highly future-shaping events. Little else does so much to shape our approach to the future than the spectacle and fallout of disaster. Disasters expand our repertoire of knowledge; like a 'fatal' computer program crash, they establish a list of 'known issues' beyond the hypothetical.

Our relationship to failure is complex and nuanced. You confidently board an airliner because of the remarkable safety record of air travel -- but this record was established largely on the backs of past failures that were subjected to rigorous investigation and scrutiny. In other words, your safety today is largely related to the learning gleaned from previous tragedies. So, even though you rightly mourn and respect the calamities of the past, you ought to find yourself appropriately appreciative and thankful for them.

Disasters are to a society what mistakes are to an individual: opportunities for adaptive improvement. Just as airplanes, sea vessels, bridges, and skyscrapers owe a great deal to previous miscalculations, so too our personal failures are highly formative experiences in our lives. We are the equations of past relationships, ventures, and mistakes.

Whether they haunt us, follow us, or teach us,
And whether we deny them, excuse them, or glean from them,
Our failures shape us.

Look for the person who has made mistakes and critically learned from them. The person who has never made a mistake is probably a con artist, or is secretly suffering from an abysmal lack of experience. Individuals who are accepting, self-aware, and critically adaptive in response to their failures make for the greatest teachers.

SPORT

Game time. We don our uniforms, tighten our cleats, and head out on to the field.

For the match to make any sense at all, both teams must agree to some fixed parameters and rules that define how points are to be scored, and what manner of conduct is appropriate for achieving these ends. Without rules, the game would not be a game at all -- just an indeterminate number of us aimlessly wandering around a field for an unset amount of time.

Included in the rules of the game, we need to reach a formal, mutual agreement that bestows authority upon an umpire, referee, or scorekeeper to declare a winner. If there is no recourse to settle a dispute over the final score except an all-out brawl, then establishing the rules serves very little purpose. As the game begins, both teams authorize this overseer to enforce the rules, and agree that overseer's adjudication of the rules will be final. A game in which a team or individual player can overturn the authority of the referee or scorer on a whim is not a game at all, just eventual chaos.

The referee is as equally bound to the rules as the players themselves. The rules define the precise scope of her authority. She cannot issue warnings, penalties, or expulsions for any behaviour save the direct violation of the rulebook that has been mutually ratified by both teams. She herself is not the law, only its enforcement. And she only exists at all because both teams need her equally.

In many respects, life itself is much like a sporting event. We instinctively know that a complete vacuum of authority would lead to absurdity, so most of us -- even if we stretch the rules to our advantage -- play the game of life cognizant of the norms that our particular society has collectively embraced.

When a crazed fan runs across the field naked and interrupts normal game play, screaming some unintelligible nonsense about the arbitrary nature of society's rules, most of us just awkwardly ignore him. We have no idea what has possessed him; we think him a lunatic, and we are quite likely to diagnose his asocial behaviour as some kind of neurological disorder. This is the power of the rulebook: if you will not (or can not) play by the rules of society, you have as little likelihood of joining in the competition as a streaker does at a soccer match.

Society, like a sporting event, only exists at all to the extent that its rules are broadly accepted as the convention by all players and referees. If you hate the rules, you may lobby for their reform. If you love the rules, you may snitch on the perpetrators who break them. But if you are like most people, you probably accept the game book as it is. If you are particularly industrious, you might also try to figure out a way to hone your performance in order to maximize your likelihood of winning given the rules, such as they are.

Then there are those who ignore the rules altogether: these are society's deviants, individuals whose actions have no reference or relationship to the mainline hierarchy of authority. Their incomprehensible behaviour meets with swift removal from the field, as security is summoned by the referees.

Like athletes, our relationship with umpires is varied, but such figures of authority represent something that we all demand: a criterion that establishes who we are with respect to others and a system that insures that our points and goals 'count' at the end of the game. If a drunk, face-painted, horn-blowing fan were allowed to run across the field and score a legitimate point in the tournament, we would madly cry foul, insisting that justice be restored to such a lawless spectacle!

Humanity without hierarchical authority structures makes as much sense as athletic events without referees or judges.

Even the most rebellious uprising or revolution is not an attempt to overthrow the essence of authority itself. Rather, it is a coordinated (though also perhaps spontaneous) effort to replace one particular authority with a different authority. At no point in communal, human existence are our lives not intertwined with jurisprudence. The game of life only makes sense if there are referees and scorekeepers involved. A revolution cries for better umpires, not for a game that is free from oversight -- for such a situation would be no game at all.

Today, if you are seeking to reform a system, institution, or situation, remember that the kernel of your ambition is ultimately the aim to transform its leadership.

ANTIFRAGILE

There is another sacred bird, too, whose name is phoenix. I myself have never seen it, only pictures of it; for the bird seldom comes into Egypt: once in five hundred years, as the people of Heliopolis say. (Herodotus 73)

The mythological Phoenix, it was said, was reborn from its own ashes when it died. Its demise led to its rebirth; its conclusion incited a new beginning:

Straightway the life spirit surges through his scattered limbs; the renovated blood floods his veins. The ashes show signs of life; they begin to move though there is none to move them, and feathers clothe the mass of cinders. He who was but now the sire comes forth from the pyre the son and successor; between life and life lay but that brief space wherein the pyre burned. (Claudian, Carmina Minora XLIV)

In Greek mythology, the multi-headed Lernaean Hydra serpent was said to grow two new heads every time one head was lost, making it such a formidable adversary that even mighty Hercules required assistance in order to destroy it:

And when one head was cut off, the place where it was severed put forth two others; for this reason it was considered to be invincible, and with good reason, since the part of it which was subdued sent forth a two-fold assistance in its place. (Diodorus Siculus, Library of History 4. 11. 5)

The Phoenix and the Hydra are creatures that benefit from volatility, risk, and disorder. They are not simply robust or resilient; they do not merely "bounce back" from devastating situations. Rather, they grow stronger as a result of adversity and stress. They gain from disaster.

Fragility, says Nassim Nicholas Taleb (b. 1960), is anything that is liable to be harmed by stress. Like a delicate ornament; the more likely that a system is to collapse or break under pressure the more fragile it is considered to be. So what is the opposite of fragility? Taleb argues that 'antifragile' systems benefit from disorder: like culture, technology, cities, and things that must, by necessity, evolve over time. These become better, stronger, and more adaptive as they undergo one crisis after another.

Crisis, then, is a necessary ingredient for the life and wellbeing of complex systems. If you comfortably lay in bed for weeks on end your muscles will atrophy. But if you spend a lot of time lifting heavy things and tear the muscle tissue you become stronger as a result of the stress. Likewise, Taleb argues, if you 'fragilize' the economy by prioritizing its stability and predictability above all else, you inadvertently make it more susceptible to systemic collapse; whereas embracing long term, unpredictable volatility fosters the formation of interdependent networks that maximize the opportunities of disturbances when they occur.

"Wind extinguishes a candle and energizes fire," writes Taleb. "You want to be the fire and wish for the wind." (Taleb 2012:3) One thing is certain: storms will come. The lasting fruit of our labour is, like the phoenix, what arises from the ashes after the dust settles.

THE UNENVISAGED

The unenvisaged situation or event is the thing we cannot predict
We have no inkling of its potential, no capacity to sense its arrival
It is entirely outside of our ability to anticipate

In economics, it brings the unintended consequence
In law, it requires an amendment to the legislation
In science, it overturns the widely accepted hypothesis

It is going to happen, but we cannot see it coming
At present, we do not possess even the smallest hint of its approaching
No foreboding, no forewarning; completely off the radar

So much of our lives are dedicated to knowing and planning
The unknown is a threat that we want to bury and deny
So much easier to assume we know everything
than to reckon with the crippling awareness that we are flying blind

But if we have learned one thing from the past thus far
is it not the awareness that we are not, in fact, omniscient?
How do we justify our trust in long-term strategic plans
while mocking the carrier of the cardboard doomsday sign?
Who knows the future, truly?

Today's ratified statement is tomorrow's target of scrutiny
And again, tomorrow, we try to see the future again
in light of the oversights we made today

We will never know the unenvisaged before its time
But we can know, certainly, that it is coming
The question is, only: who will we be when it arrives?

Notes

To Be Continued

Carry on to the next chapter by subscribing to the *Caesura Letters*. Our journey continues through the realm of compelling and provocative ideas.

Subscriptions are available in multiple formats, including weekly postal letters, daily email, online or RSS feed access, as well as quarterly ebooks and paperbacks.

Subscribe at caesuraletters.com.

About the Author

James Shelley is an author, speaker, and researcher living in Ontario, Canada. In addition to composing the Caesura Letters, James also spreads his passion for curiosity and discovery through speaking engagements—ranging from academic forums, to business conferences, to spiritual retreats. To get in touch, please email contact@jamesshelley.com

BIBLIOGRAPHY

Alesina, Alberto. & Weder, Beatrice. (2002). Do Corrupt Governments Receive Less Foreign Aid?. American Economic Review. Volume 92. Sep 2002. 1126-1137.

American Society for Microbiology (2008, June 5). Humans Have Ten Times More Bacteria Than Human Cells: How Do Microbial Communities Affect Human Health?. ScienceDaily.

Andrew, R.J. (1962). Evolution of Intelligence and Vocal Mimicking. Science, New Series. Vol 137. No. 3530. pp. 585-589.

Aristotle in 23 Volumes, Vol. 22, translated by J. H. Freese. Aristotle. Cambridge and London. Harvard University Press; William Heinemann Ltd. 1926.

Aristotle. Aristotle in 23 Volumes, Vol. 23, translated by W.H. Fyfe. Cambridge, MA, Harvard University Press; London, William Heinemann Ltd. 1932.

Armstrong, Karen. (2007). The Bible: A Biography. Vancouver: Douglas & McIntyre Ltd.

Atran, Scott. (2002). In Gods We Trust: The Evolutionary Landscape of Religion. New York: Oxford University Press.

Austin, John. (1885) Lectures on Jurisprudence, or The Philosophy of Positive Law. (5th Ed. edited by Robert Campbell). Volume I. London: John Murray.

Austin, John. (1995). The Province of Jurisprudence Determined, W. Rumble (ed.), Cambridge: Cambridge University Press.

Bagnall, Roger S. (2002). Alexandria: Library of Dreams. Proceedings of the American Philosophical Society. Vol. 146. No. 4. December 2002.

Bateson, C. Daniel. (1975). Rational Processing or Rationalization?: The Effect of Discontinuing Information on a Stated Religious Belief. Journal of Personality and Social Psychology 1975, Vol. 32, No. 1, 176-184

Bayne, Tim. (2008). The Unity of Consciousness and the Split-Brain Syndrome. The Journal of Philosophy, 105(6), 277-300.

Ben-Jacob, Eshel. Schochet, Ofer. Tenenbaum, Adam. Cohen, Inon. Czirók, Andras. & Vicsek, Tamas. (1994). Generic modelling of cooperative growth patterns in bacterial colonies. Nature 368, 46 - 49. March 3, 1994.

Berger, Peter. Luckmann, Thomas. (1966). The Social Construction of Reality: A Treatise in the Sociology of Knowledge. Double Day. (Referenced edition: 1989, Anchor Books)

Blackmore, Susan. (1999). The Meme Machine. Oxford: Oxford University Press.

Bornstein, Erica. (2001). Child Sponsorship, Evangelism, and Belonging in the Work of World Vision Zimbabwe. American Ethnologist 28(3):595-622. American Anthropological Association.

Brotton, Jeremy. (2012). A History of the World in Twelve Maps. Penguin.

Brown, Donald E. (1991). Human Universals. McGraw Hill.

Calvin, John. (1555). On the Sabbath. Part 2. On Friday the 21st of June, 1555. The 35th sermon, which is the sixth on the fifth chapter. In Sermons on Deuteronomy by John Calvin (trans. James R. Hughes)

Christian, James. (1998). Philosophy: An Introduction to the Art of Wondering, 7th ed. Orlando: Harcourt Brace College Publishers.

Claudian, Carmina Minora XXVII (XLIV). Loeb Classical Library, 1922

Connor, D. (2010). Cultural representation. In R. Jackson, & M. Hogg (Eds.), Encyclopedia of identity. (pp. 170-174). Thousand Oaks, CA: SAGE Publications, Inc

Council of Trent. (1546). Session V - Celebrated on the seventeenth day of June, 1546 under Pope Paul III, Decree concerning original sin, item 2.

Crick, Francis. (1994) The Astonishing Hypothesis: The Scientific Search for the Soul. New York: Charles Scribner's Sons.

Dawkins, Richard. (1976). The Selfish Gene. 30th Anniversary Edition (2006). Oxford: Oxford University Press.

Descartes, Rene. (1984). The Philosophical Writings of Descartes, 3 vols. (trans. John Cottingham, Robert Stoothoff, Dugald Murdoch and Anthony Kenny) Cambridge: Cambridge University Press, 1984-1991

Dryden, John. (1672). The Conquest of Granada. In Scott, Walter. (1808) The Works of John Dryden (Eighteen Volumes). Volume IV. London: Printed for William Miller, Albemarle Street. By James Ballantyne and Co. Edinburgh.

EMMA Rice Report. (2010). Port–au-Prince Rice Markets in post–earthquake Haiti.

Fadiman, Clifton. (1955). The American Treasury, 1455–1955. Harper.

Fish, Stanley. (1980). Is There a Text in this Class? The Authority of Interpretive Communities. Cambridge, Massachusetts: Harvard University Press.

Frazer, Garth. (2008). The Economic Journal. Volume 118, Issue 532, pages 1764–1784, October 2008

Giroux, Henry A., & Pollock, Grace. (2010). The Mouse that Roared: Disney and the End of Innocence. Rowman & Littlefield Publishers.

Goebl, Werner., & Palmer, Caroline. (2009). Synchronization of Timing and Motion Among Performing Musicians. Music Perception. Vol. 26. Iss. 5. pp. 427-338.

Goldthwaite, Richard A. (2009). The Economy of Renaissance Florence. Baltimore: The John Hopkins University Press.

Gutas, Dimitri. (2012). The Empiricism of Avicenna. Oriens 40. 391–436

Hacker, Frederick. (1955). Psychiatry and Religion. The Journal of Religion, Vol. 35, No. 2, Apr., 1955.

Hamilton-Baillie, Ben & Jones, Phil. (2005). Improving traffic behaviour and safety through urban design. Proceedings of ICE. Civil Engineering 158. May 2005. 39–47. Paper 14014

Harent, Stéphane. (1911). "Original Sin." In The Catholic Encyclopedia. Vol. 11. New York: Robert Appleton Company.

Harper, Gordon Lloyd. (1966). Saul Bellow, The Art of Fiction No. 37. The Paris Review. Winter 1966.

Hart, H. L. A. (1961). The Concept of Law. Oxford: Clarendon Press.

Herodotus, with an English translation by A. D. Godley. Cambridge. Harvard University Press. 1920.

Hobbes, Thomas. (1651). Of Man, Being the First Part of Leviathan. The Harvard Classics. (Edited by Charles W. Eliot). Vol. 34, Part 5, of 51. New York: P.F. Collier & Son, 1909–14.

Homer. The Odyssey with an English Translation by A.T. Murray, PH.D. in two volumes. Cambridge, MA., Harvard University Press; London, William Heinemann, Ltd. 1919.

Horneck, G., Buckner, H., & Reitz, G. (1994). Long-term survival of bacterial spores in space. Advances in Space Research. 1994. October 14(10):41-5.

Hume, David. (1889[1757]). The Natural History of Religion. London: A. and H. Bradlaugh Bonner.

Humphrey, Nicholas. (1976). The social function of the intellect. In Bateson, Paul Patrick Gordon. & Hinde, R.A. (eds.) (1976). Growing Points in Ethology. (pp. 303-317.) Cambridge: Cambridge University Press.

Humphrey, Nicholas. (2011). Soul Dust: the Magic of Consciousness. London: Quercus.

James, William. (1907). Pragmatism: a new name for some old ways of thinking. (ed. Bruce Kuklick) Indianapolis: Hackett Publishing Company. 1981.

Jabr, Ferris (2012). Does Thinking Really Hard Burn More Calories? Scientific American. July 18, 2012. http://www.scientificamerican.com/article.cfm?id=thinking-hard-calories

James, William (1899). Letter to Mrs. Henry Whitman, June 7, 1899. In James, William. (1926). The Letters of William James, ed. Henry James, vol. 2, p. 90 (1926). Kessinger Publishing reprint.

James, William. (1907). Pragmatism: a new name for some old ways of thinking. (ed. Bruce Kuklick) Indianapolis: Hackett Publishing Company. 1981.

Jefferson, Thomas. (1854). Washington, Henry Augustine. The Writings of Thomas Jefferson: Correspondence, cont. Reports and opinions while Secretary of State. Taylor & Maury.

Jevons, William Stanley. (1865). The Coal Question: An Inquiry Concerning the Progress of the Nation, and the Probable Exhaustion of Our Coal-Mines. (Cited 1866, 2nd Edition. London: Macmillan and Co.)

Jolly, Alison. (1966). Lemur Social Behavior and Primate Intelligence. Science New Series. Vol. 153. No. 3735. pp. 501-506.

Kant, Immanuel. (1799). The metaphysic of morals, divided into metaphysical elements of law and of ethics. Vol 2 of 2. London [i.e. Hamburg]

Keeley, Lawrence H. (1996). War Before Civilization: the Myth of the Peaceful Savage. Oxford University Press.

Keynes, John Maynard. (1936). The General Theory of Employment, Interest and Money. New York: Harcourt Brace and Co.

Kundera, Milan. (1991). Immortality (trans. Peter Kussi). London: Faber and Faber.

Lapidge, Michael. (2006). The Anglo-Saxon Library. Oxford University Press.

Leibniz, Gottfried (1689). New Essays on Human Understanding (Nouveaux essais sur l'entendement humain).

Leibniz, Gottfried Wilhelm Freiherr von. Clark, Samuel. (2002). Correspondence. Hackett Publishing.

Locke, John. (1836). An Essay Concerning Human Understanding. T. Tegg and Son, 1836.

Lozupone, Catherine A. Stombaugh, Jesse I. Gordon, Jeffrey I. Jansson, Janet K. & Knight Rob. (2012) Diversity, stability and resilience of the human gut microbiota. Nature 489, 220–230 (13 September 2012)

Luther, Martin. (1525). Bondage of the Will. Referenced edition: trans. Henry Cole. (2009). Digireads.com Publishing.

Luther, Martin. (1526). That These Words of Christ, 'This is my Body,' etc., Still Stand Firm Against the Fanatics. In (1961). Luther's Works, Vol. 37. Philadelphia: Fortress Press. pp. 26-27

Mandelbrot, Benoit. (1977). Fractals: Form, Chance and Dimension. W. H. Freeman.

Mallamaci, Antonello. (2011). Molecular bases of cortico-cerebral regionalization. In Gene Expression to Neurobiology and Behaviour: Human Brain Development and Developmental Disorders. Progress in Brain Research, Volume 189. Elsevier.

McGraw, A. Peter. & Warren, Caleb. (2010). Benign Violations: Making Immoral Behavior Funny. Psychological Science XX(X) 1-9

Montagu, Ashley F. (1968). Man and Aggression (Ashley Montagu, ed). New York: Oxford University Press.

Marmura, Michael. (1986). Avicenna's "Flying Man" in Context. Monist, 69:3 (July). 383-395,

Naisbitt, John (1982). Megatrends: ten new directions transforming our lives. New York: Warner Books, Inc.

Newberg, Andrew. (2009). How God Changes Your Brain: Breakthrough Findings from a Leading Neuroscientist. Random House Digital.

Payne, B. Keith. Cheng, Clara Michelle. Govorun, Olesya. & Stewart, Brandon D. (2005). An Inkblot for Attitudes: the Affect Misattribution as Implicit Measurement. Journal of Personal and Social Psychology. 2005. Vol. 89, No. 3. 277-293.

Petroski, Henry. (2004). Look First to Failure. Harvard Business Review. October 2004.

Pinker, Steven. (2004). Why nature & nurture won't go away. Dædalus. Fall 2004, 5-17.

Plato. Plato in Twelve Volumes, Vols. 5 & 6 translated by Paul Shorey. Cambridge, MA, Harvard University Press; London, William Heinemann Ltd. 1969.

Plato. Plato in Twelve Volumes, Vol. 9 translated by W.R.M. Lamb. Cambridge, MA, Harvard University Press; London, William Heinemann Ltd. 1925.

Pollan, Michael. (2013). Some of My Best Friends Are Germs. New York Times Magazine. May 15, 2013.

Prüfer, Kay., et al (2012). The bonobo genome compared with the chimpanzee and human genomes. Nature 2012/06/13/online.

Puran, Namita. (2005). Ulysses Contracts: Bound to Treatment or Free to Choose? The York Scholar. Volume 2. (Spring 2005). 42-51.

Putnam, Robert D. (1993). The Prosperous Community: Social Capital and Public Life. The American Prospect. Vol. 4 No. 13. March 21, 1993.

Rajana, Raghuram G. (2008). Aid and Growth: What Does the Cross-Country Evidence Really Show? The Review of Economics and Statistics. November 2008, Vol. 90, No. 4, pp. 643-665

Rajana, Raghuram G. & Subramanianb, Arvind. (2011). Aid, Dutch disease, and manufacturing growth. Journal of Development Economics. Volume 94, Issue 1, January 2011, Pages 106–118

Rives, Stanford. (2008). Did Calvin Murder Servetus? Infinity.

Roller, Matthew B. (2008). The consul(ar) as exemplum: Fabius Cunctator's paradoxical glory. For Beck, H. & Pina Polo (ads) Consuls, consulars, and the government of the Roman republic.

Rousseau, Jean-Jacques. (1763). Emile: or, On education. (referenced edition Basic Books, 1979)

Rudd, Melanie. Vohs, Kathleen D. & Aaker, Jennifer. (2012). Awe Expands People's Perception of Time, Alters Decision Making, and Enhances Well-Being. Psychological Science October 2012 vol. 23 no. 10: 1130-1136

Ryan, Christopher., Jethá, Cacilda. (2010). Sex at dawn: the prehistoric origins of modern sexuality. Harper.

Ryle, Gilbert. (1949). The Concept of Mind. Great Britain: William Brendon and Sons Ltd.

Sadrieh, Abdolkarim. (2010). The Selten School of Behavioral Economics: A Collection of Essays in Honor of Reinhard Selten. Springer.

Salimpoor, Valorie N. Benovoy, Mitchel. Larcher, Kevin. Dagher, Alain. & Zatorre, Robert J. (2011). Anatomically distinct dopamine release during anticipation and experience of peak emotion to music. Nature Neuroscience. Volume 14. No. 2. February 2011. pp. 257-262

Schultz, Daniel. Lu, Mingyang. Stavropoulos, Trevor. Onuchic, Jose. & Ben-Jacob, Eshel. (2013). Turning Oscillations Into Opportunities: Lessons from a Bacterial Decision Gate. Nature. 3, 1668. April 17, 2013.

Senge, Peter. Scharmer, C Otto. Jaworski, Joseph. Flowers, Betty Sue. (2005). Presence: An Exploration of Profound Change in People, Organizations, and Society. New York: Doubleday.

Shelburne, Walter A. (1988). Mythos and Logos in the Thought of Carl Jung: The Theory of the Collective Unconscious in Scientific Perspective. SUNY Press.

Simon, Herbert Alexander. (1956[1954]). Rational Choice and the Structure of the Environment. Psychological Review Vol. 63, No. 2. March 1956. pp. 129-138

Simon, Herbert Alexander. (1957). Models of man: social and rational; mathematical essays on rational human behavior in society setting. Wiley.

Smith, Cedric M. (2005). Origin and Uses of Primum Non Nocere — Above All, Do No Harm! The Journal of Clinical Pharmacology. Volume 45, Issue 4, 371–377, April 2005

Smith, David Livingstone. (2009). The Most Dangerous Animal: Human Nature and the Origins of War. Macmillan.

Soen, Yoav. Cohen, Netta. Lipson, Doron. & Braun, Erez. (1999). Emergence of spontaneous rhythm disorders in self-assembled networks of heart cells. Physical Review Letters, Vol. 82, Num. 17 , 26 April 1999, pp. 3556-3559. American Institute of Physics.

Sperber, Dan. (1996). Explaining Culture: A Naturalistic Approach. Blackwell.

Stengel, Richard. (2008). Mandela: His 8 Lessons of Leadership. TIME Magazine, Wednesday, Jul. 09, 2008.

Stillman, William James. (2005[1896]). Old Italian Masters. Kessinger Publishing.

Taleb, Nassim Nicholas. (2012). Antifragile: things that gain from disorder. New York: Random House.

Thorpe, I. J. N. (2003). Anthropology, archaeology, and the origin of warfare. World Archaeology. Vol. 35(1): 145–165. The Social Commemoration of Warfare

Tornell, Aaron. & Lane, Philip R. (1999). The Voracity Effect. The American Economic Review, Vol. 89, No. 1 (Mar., 1999), pp. 22-46

Turnbaugh, Peter J. Ley, Ruth E. Hamady, Micah. Fraser-Liggett, Claire M. Knight, Rob. & Gordon, Jeffrey I. (2007). The Human Microbiome Project. Nature. Volume 449. (October 18, 2007)

Tversky, Amos. & Kahneman, Daniel. (1974). Judgment under Uncertainty: Heuristics and Biases. Science, New Series, Vol. 185, No. 4157 (Sep. 27, 1974), pp. 1124-1131

Tversky, Amos. & Kahneman, Daniel. (1981). The Framing of Decisions and the Psychology of Choice. Science, New Series, Vol. 211, No. 4481 (Jan. 30, 1981), pp. 453-458

Vanderbilt, Tom. (2008). The Traffic Guru. The Wilson Quarterly. Summer 2008. 26-32

Vasari, Giorgio. (1946[1550]). Vasari's Lives of the Artists: The Classic Biographical Work on the Greatest Architects, Sculptors and Painters of the Italian Renaissance. (Ab. ed. Betty Burroughs). A Clarion Book. New York: Simon and Schuster.

Wiley, Tatha. (2002). Original Sin: Origins, Developments, Contemporary Meanings. New Jersey: Paulist Press.

Zwingli, Huldrich. (1530). An Account of the Faith of Hulderich Zwingli Submitted to the Roman Emperor Charles (July 3, 1530). In Macauley, S. M. (trans). (1922). The Latin Works and Correspondence of Huldreich Zwingli, vol. 2. Philadelphia: Heidelberg Press, pp. 42-56.

www.ingramcontent.com/pod-product-compliance
Lightning Source LLC
Chambersburg PA
CBHW032004190326
41520CB00007B/358